Saints, scholars, and schizophrenics revisited: A twenty-first century perspective on religion and mental health in Ireland

Michael J. Breslin & Emma Best

Copyright © 2013 Author Name Michael J. Breslin & Emma Best

All rights reserved.

ISBN-10: 149092356X
ISBN-13: 978-1490923567

Contents

Introduction		1
1	Saints, Scholars and Schizophrenics	7
2	The Benefits of Religion to Mental Health	15
3	Empirical Evidence	29
4	Schizophrenia	34
5	Schizophrenia and Religion	39
6	Schizotypy	44
7	Measuring Schizotypy	49
8	Measuring Religion	52
9	Relationship between Schizotypy and Religion	56
10	Methodology	62
11	Relationship between Religion and Mental Health	67
12	Religious Practice in Ireland	76
13	Conclusion	82
14	References	89

About the Authors

Michael Breslin holds a BSc (Hons) and a PhD in psychology both obtained from the University of Ulster at Magee. He worked as a part-time lecturer at the University of Ulster for three years. He currently works as a freelance researcher and part-time Employment Officer in Co. Donegal. He has conducted extensive research in the area of religion and mental health and has several peer reviewed publications. He has also co-edited a special issue of an academic journal on religion and mental health and occasionally acts as a reviewer for several academic journals.

Emma Best holds a BA (Hons) in Literature and Philosophy from Middlesex University, an MA in Social and Political Thought from the University of Sussex and an MSc in Computing and Information Systems from the University of Ulster. She is currently employed as a freelance music teacher.

Acknowledgements

The authors wish to thank Professor Gordon Claridge for permission to use the O-Life SF measure of schizotypy. We would also like to thank Professor Christopher Alan Lewis for all his past support. Additionally we would like to thank Ross Breslin for his encouragement to persist with this project.

Introduction

In the past when people asked what we were researching they always seemed fascinated when we told them religion and mental health. They all had a view on what the outcome was likely to be, with many people believing that religion has positive effects on mental health and others believing the opposite. Apart from the obvious benefits of religion such as social support many would think that a religious experience must be a life-changing event and if a person had such an experience then they would be filled with a sense of meaning, hope, wonder, awe, reverence and various other positive emotions that would enhance mental health.

Two areas that have recently aroused interest in religious or spiritual matters are the subjects of near death experience and angels. A plethora of literature has been produced on both of these topics. A search of Amazon using either the search term 'near death experience' or 'angels' returned thousands of results, which gives an indication of the level of interest in these phenomena. The literature written on both of these topics suggests that having some kind of a religious experience is beneficial to mental health, which in turn suggests that being religious is beneficial to mental health.

Looking first at the near death experience, it entails various combinations of an out of body experience, travelling through a tunnel, a life review, a feeling of great peace, seeing a bright light, meeting with relatives and/or spiritual beings and a reluctance to return to the world of the living. A recent book on near death experiences in Ireland (Keane, 2009) documented various mystical and visionary experiences which profoundly enhanced and enriched people's lives and also resulted in most of them becoming deeply spiritual, more concerned for others, and more interested in the meaning of life.

As well as near death experiences many books have also been written on the subject of angels. Some of these books may be exploitative but some have very inspiring stories contained within. The Big Book of Angels (Schuman, 2003) includes a story recounted by a hospital care assistant. In this story she tells of a three year old boy who was admitted to her ward. This boy had suffered terrible abuse and sustained serious physical injuries including a shattered skull. She wanted to go and say a silent prayer over the boy but the ward was too busy and chaotic. Later that day she walked by the door of the boy's room to say a prayer when suddenly she had a vision. The ceiling vanished and there were angels everywhere. She experienced an immense sense of love and joy. She saw the little boy ascend a ramp to heaven with an angel on each side holding his hand. Then an angel radiating joy approached the care assistant and told her not to worry and that the boy was going home now. When the vision passed the care assistant was told that the boy had passed away. Another story tells of an adolescent who was attempting suicide by taking pills when she heard an angel's voice telling her that she had things to do later in life and it was important that she stayed alive. Such literature suggests that people having these experiences always have a much more positive and healthy outlook on life afterwards.

Stories such as the above would suggest that religion is beneficial for mental health. Of course some would argue that anyone who has had such experiences suffers from mental health problems, most likely schizophrenia, more about this later in the book. These stories are anecdotal and science generally does not concern itself with anecdote and tends to only give serious consideration to empirical evidence. The aim of this book therefore is to examine the empirical evidence concerning the relationship between religion and mental health.

When talking about our research a few people asked us if we had read the book Saints, Scholars and Schizophrenics as though it was the definitive work on religion and mental health in Ireland. Their view was that since its publication everyone knows that religion has deleterious effects on mental health. Consequently we thought the best place to begin the research published in this book was to revisit the book Saints, Scholars and Schizophrenics by Nancy Scheper-Hughes. Just as Scheper-Hughes made anthropological research accessible to the general reader it is hoped that this book will make psychological research similarly accessible. Among other things, this book sets out to investigate Scheper-Hughes' contention that there is a positive association between religion and schizophrenia in Ireland. The book also explores the relationship between other aspects of mental health and religion, investigates the association between alcohol and mental health, and examines the prevalence of religious practice in Ireland at present.

After reviewing Scheper-Hughes' findings on the negative effects of religion on mental health in chapter 1, chapter 2 continues with an examination of some of the theories about the ways in which religion might impact mental health both positively and negatively. Chapter 3 provides a review of some of the more interesting empirical studies on the relationship between religion and mental health. Chapter 4 examines the nature of schizophrenia and explores whether the condition is best explained by the medical model. Chapter 5 looks at the relationship between schizophrenia and religion and how this relationship has

Introduction

changed with the decline of religion. Chapter 6 examines the construct of schizotypy and explores its relationship with schizophrenia. Within psychological research it is very important to describe in detail any measures employed, consequently chapter 7 examines how schizotypy is measured and describes how it is measured in this study. Chapter 8 discusses differences between religion and spirituality and describes how being religious is measured in this study. Chapter 9 reviews previous research on schizotypy and describes the other measures employed in the study. Chapter 10 looks at the methodology employed in the study and explains, for the interested reader, the statistical analyses employed in the results section. Chapter 11 reports the findings of the study in relation to measures of schizotypy, mental health, happiness, and physical health (the mental health variables) and discusses the implications of these findings. Specifically, Catholics and atheists were compared on the mental health variables. The differences between Irish respondents and U.S.A. respondents on these variables were also examined. In addition, the relationship between alcohol consumption and the mental health variables was examined. Chapter 12 reports the findings of the study in relation to the prevalence of religious practice in Ireland and discusses the implications of these findings. Chapter 13 draws conclusions from the findings and discusses the limitations of the study.

Chapter 1

Saints, Scholars and Schizophrenics

In the controversial and award winning book, Saints, Scholars, and Schizophrenics, Nancy Scheper-Hughes (2001), a social anthropologist, examined the relationship between sociocultural factors, including religion, and mental health, specifically schizophrenia, in rural Ireland. The title of her book reflects the fact that when she conducted her study she found mental illness to be very common in the land of saints and scholars. Ireland was known as the land of saints and scholars from the seventh until the twelfth century because during this period Irish priests and scholars collected and produced a vast body of books on lore and poetry and built monasteries, schools and libraries while the rest of Europe languished in the barbarism of the dark ages (Scherman, 1981). Scheper-Hughes believed that the saints, scholars and schizophrenics of Ireland were all culture bearers of the same tradition.

In 1974 Scheper-Hughes went to live for a year in what she describes as a representative small, isolated, rural community with a population of 461, in Dingle, County Kerry. To protect the anonymity of the villagers, she named the small township Ballybran and asserted that there were hundreds of villages like Ballybran throughout western Ireland (Scheper-Hughes, 2001).

Scheper-Hughes employed ethnographic methodology. She collected data through participant observation, recording field notes, conducting interviews, and administering projective tests including the Thematic Apperception Tests to facilitate storytelling. She described her work as the first ethnographic study to explore "the meanings of going and being mad" in Ireland (Scheper-Hughes, 2001; p. 35).

Citing World Health Organisation and Irish psychiatric hospital statistics Scheper-Hughes pointed out that in 1974 the Irish had the highest rates of first admission to mental hospitals in the world, particularly for schizophrenia. Additionally, on a census day in 1971 two percent of males in Western Ireland were in mental hospitals. The prevalence of schizophrenia in Ireland was nearly double the rate suggested as a norm for Western societies. Since research showed that American psychiatrists were much more likely to make a diagnosis of schizophrenia than psychiatrists from the British Isles it was unlikely that Ireland's schizophrenia statistics had been inflated by misdiagnosis. Furthermore, Irish emigrants and their descendants had psychiatric rates that far exceeded other ethnic groups (Scheper-Hughes, 2001).

Saints, Scholars and Schizophrenics

Despite this, Scheper-Hughes argued that the inflated rates of schizophrenia may have been the result of people suffering from transient psychosis being too readily labelled as schizophrenic. She suggested that this labelling process had its origins in the moral judgements of Irish villagers who were content to see people who did not conform to their idea of normal behaviour consigned to various institutions. She believed that a society reveals itself most clearly in the phenomena it rejects and excludes. Read (2004a) concurred, arguing that one of the functions of treatment for people with schizophrenia is to supress behaviours that are unacceptable to individuals with the power to enforce social norms.

Scheper-Hughes (2001) argued that, compared to the 1970s, many psychiatrists now accept that schizophrenia is a crude diagnostic label to describe a cluster of symptoms that may represent more than one mental illness. She suggested that since she observed value conflicts and threats to social self-identity among her participants she expected a change in diagnosis from schizophrenia to depression. Furthermore, since the Irish were hospitalized twelve times as often as the English for alcoholism (Scheper-Hughes, 2001) depression may be under-diagnosed in Ireland. Scheper-Hughes argued that a certain level of mental illness is tolerated in Ireland when it is disguised under the cloak of alcohol. To this extent alcoholism is a safer form of pathology than many other forms of mental illness including schizophrenia. Scheper-Hughes' contention suggests that Irish people may use alcohol as a form of self-medication. There is some support for this since alcohol, and substance abuse generally, have been linked with mental health disorders. The reasons why alcohol misuse and mental health problems might co-occur include: 1) people with mental health problems may self-medicate with alcohol; 2) the misuse of alcohol may lead to mental health problems; and 3) some third variable, such as personality traits or environmental conditions, leads to both alcohol misuse and mental health problems (Reedy & Kobayashi, 2012).

Irish people are among the highest alcohol consumers in Europe with 54% of Irish respondents binge-drinking at least once a week, compared to 28% of Europeans. In Ireland 34% usually consume at least five drinks (equivalent to two-and-a-half pints) per drinking occasion while only 10% of EU citizens consume this amount. Binge drinking is associated with adverse health outcomes including depression and suicide. For example, alcohol-related disorders were ranked as the third most common reason for admission to Irish psychiatric hospitals in 2005. Ireland has also the highest proportion of abstainers, suggesting even higher rates of alcohol consumption among Irish drinkers

Saints, Scholars and Schizophrenics

compared to their European counterparts (Mongon et al., 2007).

During the period when Scheper-Hughes conducted her study she indicated that the possible Irish vulnerability to schizophrenia was treated as an embarrassing national scandal and a stain on cultural identity. For the next twenty years following the publication of her book the validity and reliability of the statistics indicating high rates of schizophrenia were the subject of debate. More recent psychiatric hospital records showed a decline for new admissions for schizophrenia mainly as the result of a policy of deinstitutionalization which began to take effect in the 1980s (Scheper-Hughes, 2001).

In 1961 Ireland had one of the highest psychiatric rates in the world with 7.3 per 1000 of the population registered in psychiatric hospitals, with schizophrenia accounting for the highest proportion of patients. There was a 78% reduction in hospitalization rates for schizophrenia between 1971 and 2001. By 2002 there was an 80% reduction in psychiatric patients generally. However, the rate still remained one of the highest in the world. Factors that have impacted the decrease in registered psychiatric patients include: death and non-replacement, transferring patients to specialized facilities for people with an intellectual disability, the re-designation of some parts of hospitals as non-

Religion and Mental Health in Ireland

psychiatric, the establishment of community alternatives to in-patient treatment such as day care, home care and community-based interventions. For example, by 2001 there were over 3,000 community-based residential places provided for psychiatric patients (Walsh & Daly, 2004). In 1974 when Scheper-Hughes conducted her research hospitalization rates for schizophrenia was 252.8 per 100,000 (Walsh & Daly, 2004), while in 2009 hospitalization rates for schizophrenia-related disorders was 18 per 100,000 (Daly: personal communication, January 2011), a fourteen-fold decrease on 1974 rates.

Scheper-Hughes believed that religion was a major contributor to mental illness in Ireland. The importance of religion to her participants was reflected in a measure administered to forty-eight secondary school pupils. They were asked to rank order twenty-one occupations from the most to the least important. Results indicated that for females a priest was the second most important occupation, a doctor being first. For males a priest was the fourth most important occupation, once again a doctor being first.

Scheper-Hughes argued that Irish Catholic values of monastic asceticism contributed to long-term institutionalization for mental health problems. She pointed out that such values demand solitude, silence, seclusion, celibacy, fasting and self-mortification. She suggested that

Saints, Scholars and Schizophrenics

this tradition has left an indelible mark on the personality of the Irish Catholic. She pointed out that the ideology of the early Irish monks was perpetuated by priests, school teachers, and parents who instilled in young people a disdain for sex and family life and a greater respect for being socially isolated than for being a group member. She suggested that Irish Catholicism fostered a tradition of sexual repression, fear of intimacy, mistrust of love, distrust of reason, worry about sin and damnation, and glorification of self-mortification, all of which contributed to high rates of mental illness. She reported that Roman Catholics in Northern Ireland were hospitalized twice as often as Protestants for schizophrenia and three times as often for alcoholism. In her own study, the clinical histories of psychiatric patients showed a greater tendency towards delusions of a religious nature as opposed to secular delusions which were common among American schizophrenics. Furthermore, she suggested that Catholic scrupulosity might prevent psychiatric patients from discussing repressed feelings and desires with their doctors or psychiatrists. If such discussions took place then the patients may later suffer from strong feelings of guilt. She argued that many Irish psychiatrists see religious guilt as a contributory factor to mental illness.

Although Scheper-Hughes presents a credible argument for a negative association between religion and

Religion and Mental Health in Ireland

mental health, she provides no correlational evidence that might suggest such a causal relationship exists. She concedes that the evidence that ethnography produces is subjective and as such is not scientific. However, as she implies in her book, like an artist she painted a picture of rural Ireland the way she saw it. Her findings in relation to high rates of schizophrenia in Ireland are still cited in psychology text books (e.g. Kowalski & Westen, 2011).

The aims of this book were to examine the prevalence of religious practice in Ireland, to examine the relationship between religion and mental health, and to ascertain if there was any relationship between religion, specifically Catholicism, and schizophrenia as suggested by Scheper-Hughes. Another aim was to compare the mental health of Irish respondents with U.S.A. respondents with a view to examining Scheper-Hughes' (2001) claim that the Irish had psychiatric rates that far exceeded other ethnic groups. A further aim was to investigate the relationship between alcohol and mental health variables with a view to examining Scheper-Hughes' (2001) claim that a certain level of mental illness is tolerated in Ireland when it is disguised under the cloak of alcohol.

Chapter 2

The Benefits of Religion to Mental Health

In the last chapter we explored how religion might have deleterious effects on mental health. It is also pertinent to examine what the salutary effects of religion on mental health might be and we do that in this chapter. Levine (2008) pointed out that religion may be beneficial to psychological well-being for a number of reasons including: a) God may be conceptualized as a key member of an individual's support group and this can relieve distress; b) God may be viewed as an attachment figure in a similar way to a parent and this can lead to a reduction in feelings of loneliness and an increase in feelings of calmness and security; c) placing the problem in God's hands can result in relinquishing control of uncontrollable events and this can lead to a reduction in stress; d) praying to God may not change an individual's situation but it may change for the better the way they appraise their situation; and e) the practice of prayer may result in positive physiological and psychological changes similar to the positive effects of meditation (Ricard, 2007). Breslin and Lewis (2008) conducted a review on how religion, specifically prayer, might benefit mental and physical health. They concluded that: (a) religion may improve health because of the placebo effect; (b) people who are religious may also engage in health-related behaviour such as refraining from smoking, drinking, taking drugs and other risky behaviour; (c) religion may help by diverting attention from health problems; (d) prayer may promote health through supernatural intervention by God, but this is not amenable to scientific testing; (e) prayer may activate latent energies, such as chi, which have not been empirically verified, but which nevertheless may be beneficial to health; and (f) religion may result in a unity of consciousness which facilitates the transmission of healing between individuals, for example, when an individual or group pray(s) for healing for a person. Again there is no empirical evidence for this latter postulate.

Being religious relates to how a person creates a sense of meaning in their lives. Religion may provide meaning in people's lives by allowing them to view the bigger picture. Without religion a person might adapt a materialistic approach to life whereby they become frustrated if they are unable to gratify their personal needs and wishes. If a person accepts a transcendent reality they may believe that major events such as birth and death are merely signposts along a much longer developmental process. This broader meaning to life might allow people to cope with stressful events and to find personal stability even during periods of emotional pain and suffering. Surveys have shown that 70 to 80 percent of patients with psychiatric disorders use religious beliefs and activities to cope with their daily difficulties and frustrations. Research also suggests that religion may have a small protective effect against suicide but should not be overestimated in the context of other risk factors (Piedmont, 2009; Hefti, 2009; Braam, 2009).

In terms of brain neurology, religious activities such as prayer or meditation have been found to increase levels of serotonin and dopamine. Increased levels of serotonin may help alleviate depression while increased levels of dopamine may have deleterious effects on schizophrenic patients (Perroud, 2009).

Religion might be beneficial to mental health because of the amount of ritual involved in religious practice. Ritual is a symbolic activity that is carried out in order to achieve some desired outcome. Research suggests that performing rituals leads to feelings of control which in turn can lead to a reduction in negative emotions (Norton & Gino, 2013). This sense of control over negative emotions may be beneficial to mental health. Curiously, people who do not believe in rituals can also benefit from the increased sense of control that they bestow. Additionally, the effects of a ritual are not dependent upon the specific acts of the ritual since different religions have different ritualistic behaviours to mark similar events. For example, Hindus stress the removal of hair while mourning while growing a beard is the preferred ritual for Jewish males (Norton & Gino, 2013). Although it appears that ritualistic behaviour can be beneficial to mental health, it has to be remembered that behaviour which is overly ritualistic such as obsessive-compulsive disorder (OCD) can be detrimental to mental health (Norton & Gino, 2013).

Although there is some evidence for the benefits of religion to mental health, the mechanisms by which this happens still have to be clarified. For example, if a study finds that church attendance is good for mental health this may be the result of social networking and social support rather than spiritual reasons. There are different views on the ways in which religion might impact mental health. There follows a review of some of the more prominent theories on the subject.

Freud (1949) believed that religion first developed through the humanization of nature. Natural elements were assigned human-like passions so people could better understand and come to terms with the vicissitudes of nature. Primitive humans projected their existence onto the world and regarded all observed events as the manifestation of beings who fundamentally resembled human beings. This developed into the notion that everything that happens in the world expresses the intentions of a superior Intelligence and is ultimately for our own good, even if it does not appear so to us. Humans then generalized the notion that the moral laws which govern this world also govern the whole universe. Freud believed that religion had a negative impact on mental health. He characterized religion as a universal neurosis and viewed religious beliefs as damaging to the individual and to society generally. He regarded religion as a regression to childhood when the helpless infant lacked the capacity to deal with a hostile environment and needed the protection of a father who was perceived to be all-powerful. Just as the child fears the father but also relies on him for protection against known dangers so too the adult fears and depends on God and establishes an intimate and intense relationship similar to the one the child experienced with the father. He believed that these childhood wishes are unconsciously projected onto reality, creating an image of God that reflects the image of the father. He argued that the longing for the father was the root of the need for religion. He suggested that the consolation offered by religion could be compared to the effects of a narcotic drug and religious people become dependent on these effects.

Even if Freud was correct, religion may still have beneficial effects on mental health. For example, within the school of Self psychology (Kohut, 1977), which builds on Freudian theory, poor mental health can be understood in terms of unmet developmental needs. The child does not experience the caregiver as separate and independent from the self and has a need for a certain unity with the caregiver (Kohut, 1977). As infants grow and differentiate themselves from caregivers this need for unity diminishes but never disappears. Healthy adults are able to pursue this need for unity in a more differentiated way. One way this need may be met is through religious beliefs, to the extent that the adult can merge with an idealized omnipotent caregiver, namely God, in the same way that the infant merges with the caregiver (Knabb & Newgren, 2011). Consequently, religion may have beneficial effects on mental health.

Unlike Freud, Jung (2001) believed that religion was beneficial to mental health. He viewed the absence of religion as the main cause of psychological disorders among adults (Hall, Francis, & Callaghan, 2011). Jung (2001) argued that neuroses are caused by individuals ignoring their religious promptings because of a naive desire for rationality. He believed that religion gave meaning and purpose to life and set people free from internal conflict. He even claimed that the problems of all his patients over the age of 35 could be ascribed to their inability to find a religious outlook on life.

Jung believed that religion was a positive outlet for psychic energy which needed to be expressed in some way. He believed that there was an underlying psychic reality.

This psychic reality included the experience of our own unconscious i.e., all the processes of instinct, imagery, feelings and energy that occur within us and among us without our direct knowledge (Ulanov, 1997). Jung (2001) equated the unconscious with the spirit and he argued that the unconscious is the source of all conscious thoughts including the idea of life after death. The collective unconscious is the unconscious that is shared by everyone. People are impelled towards spirituality because of the structure of the collective unconscious (Chung & Hyland, 2012). As they become consciously aware of the power and influence of the unconscious and sense the psychic energy flowing within and around them, people understand this to be an aspect of God. Jung argued that the unconscious was not itself God but a medium through which God speaks (Ulanov, 1997). Jung referred to such divine manifestations as numinous experiences and he believed they were beneficial to mental health. He believed that it was only through the revelation of wisdom greater than their own that people could be lifted out of their psychological distress (Jung, 2001).

Jung referred to the forces within the unconscious, through which God may speak, as the Self. In Jung's view, the Self possesses its own independent life. This unconscious part of the individual may plan events that the conscious part perceives negatively. However, it can be beneficial to mental health if people accept the wisdom of what the unconscious part (the Self) is planning for them. This is similar to believing that this is God's will or this is karma. Additionally, the Self produces images to balance people's conscious one-sidedness so that they can include all sides of their personality as they attempt to become integrated individuals (Corbett, 1996).

Corbett (1996) argued that religion, particularly religious experience, facilitated the expression of psychic energy and acted like an underground spring which sustained life and gave it meaning. He suggested that religious dogma, viewed as shared dreams of humanity, offered protection against intense and troubling numinous experiences by allowing people to fit such experiences within the religious framework. Because of this, religion is beneficial to mental health. If people are allowed to add their own numinous experiences to the inherited religious symbols then the religious tradition can develop; if not then it can decay. Numinous experiences are often presented in a way that is relevant to the developmental history of the experiencer, often address the experiencer where s/he is most wounded, and can often result in a positive reorganisation of the personality and a deepening of sense of identity (Corbett, 1996). To put this in context, throughout our research we have come across people who have stories about extraordinary things happening at a time in their lives when they were most vulnerable. For example a complete stranger approaching them and saying something wise, profound and helpful which relates directly to the situation in which they find themselves. This could be described as a numinous experience and is sometimes viewed as God moving in a mysterious way.

Jung (2001, p. 211) believed that "... religion has grown suspect ..." and he argued that it was necessary that people rediscovered the life of the spirit. He claimed that religions no longer appear to come from within, are no longer expressions of people's psychic lives, and no longer teach people how to reconcile themselves with their own nature. Corbett (1996) agreed, arguing that religion has become de-spiritualized. He suggested that the recent failure of religion to facilitate any proper connection to psychic reality may have resulted in the psychic energy assuming negative forms that can lead to a sense of hopelessness, neurosis or psychosis. Jung believed that religious symbols are no longer effective as indicators of divine presence and people are now left on their own to deal with aspects of the divine in whatever form they take (Ulanov, 1997). Mercer (2011) provided support for this contention, pointing out that young people project their deep longings for communion with

Divinity onto cultural images such as vampire characters in fictional romantic teenage literature.

Religious traditions such as Buddhism promote the practice of mindfulness, which may be beneficial to mental health. Mindfulness is a practice whereby the practitioner lets go of worries and concerns, pays careful attention to events in the present moment, acknowledging thoughts but not dwelling on them. In Christianity mindfulness is also encouraged, for example "consider the lilies of the field, how they grow: they neither toil nor spin …. do not worry about tomorrow, for tomorrow will worry about its own things" (Matthew 6:25-34). Within psychotherapy and counselling, mindfulness-based interventions are increasingly perceived to be beneficial to mental health (Malinowski, 2008).

Schumaker (1995) argued that religion was good for mental health on two fronts. Firstly, religions are able to disguise mental disorders such as schizophrenia. According to Schumaker, many of history's best evangelists were schizophrenic or otherwise psychotic and many saints underwent religious conversions as a result of what would now be considered psychopathology, including St. Teresa, St. Paul, and St. Thérèse. In the past if certain people claimed to have heard the voice of God they were regarded as potential saints, today they might be regarded as insane. Schumaker pointed out that culture is a fine line separating religion from many forms of psychopathology and when bizarre beliefs lose their social sanction they become clinical symptoms rather than religious certainties.

Secondly, religion allows people to construct alternative versions of reality that are more conducive to positive mental health than the reality they encounter by way of strictly rational cognitive processes. The psychologically healthy person does not necessarily see things as they are, rather they see things as they would like them to be. People are less likely to suffer from psychological disorders as they become more adept at self-deception since research evidence shows that reality can be depressing (Schumaker, 1995). Religion allows people to see things as they would like them to be. Several studies report that reality-distortion and self-deception are beneficial to mental health (Schumaker, 1995). Schumaker argued that religion evolved for reasons of survival and enhanced coping. Evolution uniquely bestowed on humans the ability to regulate their own reality and to translate it into a more acceptable form. Schumaker believed that although religion can be good for mental health it is still pathological. He argued that psychopathology does not cease to be psychopathology simply because large groups of people happen to participate in it.

Schumaker posited that when humans evolved the ability to dissociate, religion became possible. In dissociation the brain can disengage itself in such a way as to block a conclusion that would otherwise present itself in the light of available information and deliver a fabricated alternative to the rejected portions of reality. For example, a person may block awareness that there is no scientific evidence for the existence of spiritual beings while praying to a guardian angel. Or a person who loses a loved one may believe that the spirit of the loved one is with them always, even though there has never been any scientific evidence for this. Schumaker argued that if everyone distorted reality in an individual way then chaos would ensue but if people distort reality as a group then religion is born. The goal of religion is to establish delusions, at the group level, that skew reality in desired directions. Most religions establish the collective delusion that a person is being loved and cared for by an invisible spirit or God. When religion is functioning well, it can produce personal and social benefits and states of bliss, whereby a person feels that he or she is of supreme importance in the eyes of an ultimate being. Schumaker argued that if a person did not transcend and transform reality then their mental health would suffer. He proposed that religious beliefs were adaptive cognitive errors. If one person distorts reality then the rest of the population will view this as a ridiculous fabrication and are likely to see this person as insane, but if the whole population distorts reality then this is acceptable and regarded as normal. Beliefs seen as normal in a religious context would be deemed abnormal if they occurred outside the context of religion.

Schumaker believed that the human mind would quickly become overwhelmed if it dwelled only on the world of often painful facts, or what he calls primary reality. Religion translates this into a more acceptable secondary reality. If people can no longer rely on religion to do this then they are more likely to develop a personal psychopathology. For example, within a religious context prayer is an acceptable way of dealing with primary reality, but if a person does not rely on religion, then they may develop a ritualistic combination of obsessions and compulsions in order to cope with painful primary reality. Religion can improve on reality on a collective basis and, overall, the research evidence shows that religion has a positive effect on mental health (Schumaker, 1995).

To sum up, Freud believed religion was damaging to mental health because it prevents people from facing up to reality and instead encourages childish notions. Jung viewed the absence of religion as one of the main causes of mental health problems because religion allows people to tap into a wisdom greater than their own which provides guidance and therefore alleviates psychological distress. Schumaker argued that religion was good for mental health because it helps disguise mental disorders such as schizophrenia, and also allows people to see things as they would like them to be rather than as they actually are.

Chapter 3

Empirical Evidence

In the previous chapter we looked at how religion might be related to mental health from a theoretical perspective. In this chapter we look at some interesting empirical evidence for the relationship between religion and mental health.

There has been a considerable body of empirical research on the relationship between religion and health, including mental health. Studies range from the effects of holy water on the growth of plants (Lenington, 1979) to the effects of being prayed for on physical health (Byrd, 1988). One curious study was conducted by Charles Darwin's cousin Sir Francis Galton. Galton (1872) investigated the effects of intercessory prayer on longevity among adult males, including members of the royal family. He examined the mean age attained by males of various classes who survived their thirteenth year. The lowest mean age was found among royals, a group who were most often prayed for, leading Galton to hypothesise that being prayed for had no beneficial effect on health.

A more recent interesting study on the effects of being prayed for was conducted by Krucoff et al. (2001). They investigated the effects of noetic therapies, including intercessory prayer among coronary patients. The term noetic refers to interventions that have physiological or spiritual effects without using drugs, medical devices, or surgical procedures (Horrigan & Krucoff, 1999). Results showed that although there was a slight reduction in adverse outcomes in the noetic therapies group, compared to the control group, the difference was not statistically significant. Curiously, when a six-month follow up was conducted all mortality occurred in the noetic therapies group. In other words, the results suggested that being prayed for was bad for your health since the control group fared better. Notwithstanding this, Dawkins (2006) pointed out that experiments such as these can bring ridicule upon religion because the implication is that God cannot help certain individuals because they are members of the control group.

Several research studies found no relationship between religion and mental health (e.g., Bergan & McConatha, 2000; Francis & Gibbs, 1996; Joyce & Weldon, 1965; Lindgren & Coursey, 1995; Matthews, Conti, & Sireci, 2001; O'Connor, Cobb, & O'Connor, 2003; Sherkat & Reed, 1992; Strayhorn, Weidman, & Larson, 1990).

Some research studies have reported a negative relationship between religion and mental health. For example: Bible study was associated with higher rates of generalized anxiety disorder (Koenig et al., 1993); religious devotional activities were positively associated with depression (Ellison, 1995); frequency of prayer was positively associated with obsessionality (Lewis & Maltby, 1995), and positively associated with neuroticism (Lewis, Francis, & Enger, 2004).

Despite this, generally empirical research studies show weak to moderate correlational evidence for a positive relationship between religion and mental health, suggesting that religion is beneficial to mental health (Breslin, 2006). For example: belief in God and a more positive attitude towards Christianity were associated with higher levels of psychological well-being (Francis & Kaldor, 2002; Francis et al., 2004); personal religious devotion was inversely related to depressive symptoms and problem drinking (Kendler, Gardner, & Presscott, 1997); private religiosity was negatively associated with suicidal ideation and suicide attempts (Nonnmaker, McNeely, & Blum, 2003); church attendance was positively associated with well-being, negatively associated with depression, negatively associated with distress, and positively associated with life satisfaction (Koenig, et al., 1997; Ellison et al., 2001; Markides, 1983); prayer was positively associated with psychological well-being, purpose in life, and optimism (Poloma & Pendleton, 1991; Francis & Evans, 1996; Biggar et al., 1999); and relationship with God was positively associated with optimism (Mattis, Fontenot, & Hatcher-Kay, 2003).

Recently the concept of positive psychology has been developed to address the notion that mental health is not just an absence of illness, rather it can be viewed positively by the presence of traits that reflect good mental health. Positive psychology focuses on strengths as opposed to weaknesses. Such strengths include joy, forgiveness, gratitude, satisfaction, contentment, serenity, optimism, humour and generosity. Happiness can be cultivated by identifying and using such positive traits and this formulation of happiness leads to good mental health. Happiness also prolongs life and improves health. Research suggests that religious people are somewhat happier and more satisfied with life than non-religious people. MacLachlan and Hand (2013) reported, among an Irish sample, that religion had a small positive influence on happiness.

Religion may increase happiness because it engenders hope for the future and creates a sense of meaning in life. Research shows that the more fundamentalist the religion the more optimistic are its adherents, and the increase in optimism associated with religion is accounted for by a greater sense of hope (Seligman, 2002). Dawkins (2006) concedes that religion may have a small effect on levels of happiness but he argues that atheists have no general tendency towards unhappiness; rather they can lead happy and fulfilled lives without religion. One aim of this book was

Empirical Evidence

to add to the research literature by comparing the levels of happiness between believers and atheists.

Chapter 4

Schizophrenia

In this chapter we look at schizophrenia and examine different theoretical perspectives on the condition. Theories on schizophrenia range from the medical model which views schizophrenia as a disease caused by biological factors to perspectives whereby schizophrenia is seen as a meaningless label which ties together a group of symptoms which do not constitute a single disease.

The Diagnostic and Statistical Manual of Mental Disorders classifies schizophrenia as a psychotic disorder (APA, 2000; DSM-IV-TR). Schizophrenia is a generic term for a group of conditions which can be classified under the general heading of psychosis. It is a heterogeneous disorder and no single symptom is a defining feature (Davey, 2008). Symptoms of schizophrenia include disturbance of thought, perception and language, delusions, hallucinations, lack of motivation, socially inappropriate behaviour, and withdrawal from relationships (Kowalski & Westen, 2011). These symptoms can be conceptualized as falling into two broad categories, positive and negative. The positive symptoms reflect an excess of normal functions, while the negative symptoms reflect a diminution of normal functions. Positive symptoms include disorganised speech, delusions and

Schizophrenia

hallucinations, while negative symptoms include: loss of interest; restrictions in the range and intensity of emotional expression e.g., unresponsiveness, poor eye contact, and reduced body language; and restrictions in the initiation of goal directed behaviour. No single symptom is indicative of schizophrenia, rather the diagnosis involves various symptoms associated with impaired social or occupational functioning, or dysfunctional self-care (APA, 2000; DSM-IV-TR).

Schizophrenia can be a very debilitating disease. For example, in England people with severe mental illness such as schizophrenia die 15-20 years earlier than the general population, psychosis is related to higher levels of debt, and only 8% of people with schizophrenia are in employment. At any time a third of people in acute mental health units will have a diagnosis of schizophrenia or other psychotic illnesses (The Schizophrenia Commission, 2012).

Some believe the term 'schizophrenia' implies a split personality whereas Eugen Bleuler, the originator of the term, used it to indicate that different psychological functions were split from each other (Loewenthal, 2007). Bleuler used the term schizophrenia to refer to different forms of psychoses and the term schizophrenia is still used to denote more severe forms of psychoses (The Schizophrenia Commission, 2012). There is strong evidence that schizophrenia has a biological basis (Loewenthal 2007; Schumaker, 1995). However, Read, Mosher and Bentall (2004) strongly disagree with the biological or medical model of schizophrenia, arguing that it is not supported by research and that adverse life experience is a more plausible explanation for the onset of schizophrenia. No single biological factor is consistently found in individuals diagnosed with schizophrenia (Heinrichs, 1993) and schizophrenia cannot be diagnosed in an individual solely by a brain scan (Harrison, 1995). In about fifty percent of the pairs of identical twins in which one twin had schizophrenia the other twin was healthy, suggesting that the environment must contribute to the occurrence of schizophrenia (Lickey & Gordon, 1983). Bleuler, the originator of the term, was rather vague and ambiguous in his description of the causes, the symptoms and the potential cures of schizophrenia (Read, 2004b). Read and Mason (2004) argue that the legacy of Bleuler's work resulted in psychiatrists attaching the meaningless and socially devastating label of schizophrenia instead of attempting to unravel the confused thought processes of the mentally ill. Read (2004c) argued that schizophrenia is now a label for a range of different types of distressing behaviours.

Just about every variable known to affect human behaviour has been implicated in the cause of schizophrenia at some stage or another (Bentall, 2004). Some researchers argue that schizophrenia also has a strong genetic component and the predisposition to schizophrenia is inherited (e.g., Lickey & Gordon, 1983). In the general population the risk of schizophrenia is less than one percent. However the risk is much greater for the relatives of schizophrenics. The parents of a schizophrenic child have about a 5% risk of schizophrenia, the siblings of a schizophrenic have about a 10% risk and the children of a schizophrenic parent have a 14% chance of developing the disorder. If both parents have schizophrenia the child has a risk factor of about 50% (Beatty, 1995). Although there has been considerable research in trying to identify a schizophrenic gene or genes and a number of chromosomes have been implicated, studies of multigenerational families have found no evidence that any particular gene is linked to schizophrenia (Carlson, 2010). Moreover, genetic linkage analyses suggest that predisposition for psychotic symptoms, if indeed genetic, is not transmitted through a single gene (Davey, 2008). Most researchers now believe that many genes are involved in the susceptibility of schizophrenia. Furthermore, schizophrenia can run in families for environmental reasons such as exposure to common rearing patterns (Joseph, 2004). Evidence that it is not necessary to have a genetic predisposition to develop schizophrenia was provided by the finding that deprived children were more likely to develop schizophrenia, among children with no family history of psychosis (Read, 2004e). Adverse life events can contribute to the symptoms of schizophrenia in the same way that they contribute to other mental health problems (Davies & Burdett, 2004). Schizophrenia has been reported to occur in the range of 0.5% to 1.5% of the general population (APA, 2000; DSM-IV-TR).

To conclude, the debate as to whether schizophrenia is best understood from a medical model perspective seems set to continue for the foreseeable future. However, since antipsychotic drugs would appear to be the most effective treatment for many of the symptoms of schizophrenia (Davey, 2008) it seems that the medical model offers the patient the best prospects of leading a normal life. There are at least twenty antipsychotic drugs currently available. They work because they block dopamine receptors in the brain. While they are all effective to some extent none is completely effective in all people. Clozapine is the most effective drug but researchers are not sure why it is more effective than the other drugs (The Schizophrenia Commission, 2012).

Chapter 5

Schizophrenia and Religion

In the past schizophrenia and religion were sometimes regarded as two sides of the same coin. Schizophrenia was understood to be the result of some evil influence and approaches to treatment included prayer or sacrifice. In the Old Testament madness was held to be the result of sinning while in the New Testament Christ was revered for casting out demons (Read, 2004a). During the Middle Ages people suffering from psychosis often thought they themselves were possessed by the devil (Borras & Huguelet, 2009). Today schizophrenia and religion are seldom associated in the minds of health professionals.

Despite this, in some cases the behaviour and experience of schizophrenics appear similar to the behaviour and experience of some religious practitioners, for example in the Hindu and Buddhist traditions. In the practice of Zen Buddhism students are encouraged to sit endlessly in the same position and ponder a seemingly nonsense statement, known as a koan. A famous one is *why is a mouse when it spins*. A koan could be similar to a statement heard from a schizophrenic. The purpose of pondering a koan is to attain enlightenment, a seemingly contradictory state whereby 'to seek it is to lose it' (Watts, 1962). Similarly, very strange behaviours, exhibited by followers of the philosophy of Kundalini (a Hindu philosophy), which could be diagnosed as schizophrenia are documented by White (1990). Furthermore, many religious mystics within the Christian and Muslim traditions have described religious experiences that have parallels with schizophrenic symptomatology (cf. Merkur, 1993). The difference between individuals who engage in esoteric practices and who claim to have 'attained enlightenment' and individuals who suffer from schizophrenia would seem to be that individuals who have 'attained enlightenment' have a sense of unity within themselves, with other individuals and with the entire universe whereas individuals suffering from schizophrenia experience a split in their relationship with the world and with the self (Laing, 1990). Similarly, if a religious belief results in emotional distress, impaired behaviour or a decrease in social functioning then it is a delusion (Mohr & Pfeifer, 2009).

There may be parallels between eastern philosophy and what Gross (1996) describes as the psychedelic model of schizophrenia. In this model the schizophrenic is seen as an eloquent critic of society and schizophrenia is itself a natural way of healing the state of alienation called 'normality'. Schizophrenia is seen as a voyage into inner space from which the patient returns to the normal world with new insights. If the patient were allowed to explore their schizophrenia without the intervention of drug treatment the question is would they achieve the same degree of integration of personality as practitioners of Zen and other esoteric practices seem to achieve? The evidence to date seems to indicate that they would not.

Twenty five to thirty five percent of patients with schizophrenia encounter delusions with religious content. These religious delusions have been associated with a poorer prospect of recovery. Furthermore, they appear to be accompanied by more intense suffering than other forms of delusions. Intensive religious practice is not necessary for the onset of religious delusions but is often associated with their onset (Huguellet & Mohr, 2009; Mohr & Pfeifer, 2009).

In a review of studies on the relationship between schizophrenia and religion Miller and Kelly (2005) suggested that the content of delusions and hallucinations is a function of the cultural, political and religious climate. Specifically, if the sufferer is embedded in a religious climate they will have religious delusions; if not, they won't. Delusions in previous ages were confined to religion and with the decline of religion secular delusions emerged. Psychiatric historians have noted that prior to the twentieth century the symptoms of schizophrenia tended to be of a religious nature much more frequently than the present day (Schumaker, 1995). It would appear that thinking you are Jesus is no more symptomatic of schizophrenia than thinking you are Napoleon. Despite this, questions about the nature of a person's relationship with God are often evoked by psychotic experiences (Geekie, 2004). The British queen's mother in law claimed to be in contact with Christ and Buddha and was diagnosed with schizophrenia by two psychiatrists. Predictably, Freud believed her religious delusions were not a result of schizophrenia but a product of sexual frustration (Cohen, 2013). It is possible that all three psychiatrists were wrong and the queen's mother in law was having a bona fide religious experience. Another possibility is that people with precarious mental health are attracted to religious movements which encourage bizarre beliefs and unusual experiences (Loewenthal, 2007) and this is why some people think there is an association between religion and schizophrenia.

In the past bizarre beliefs and unusual experiences within a religious context were a way of maintaining good mental health in a world where primary reality would otherwise have adverse consequences for mental health (Schumaker, 1995) but today if a person admits to bizarre beliefs and unusual experiences, whether of a religious nature or not, they are usually considered mentally ill. With the decline in religion there has also been a decline in religious symptomatology accompanying schizophrenia, resulting in less of an association between religion and mental illness in the minds of the general population.

Chapter 6

Schizotypy

In this chapter we examine the construct of schizotypy and explore its relationship with schizophrenia.

The Diagnostic and Statistical Manual of Mental Disorders lists different categories of mental health disorders. Emil Kraeplin (1856-1926) was one of the first clinicians to categorise mental illness. He believed that different mental illnesses had different forms of biological pathology. A contemporary of Kraeplin, Eugen Bleuler (1847-1939), believed that people varied along dimensions of mental illness, rather than falling into the categories of being mentally ill or not. The notion of continua of mental health problems was used later by other psychologists who favoured a psychological rather than a medical approach to mental illness (Chung & Hyland, 2012).

Normal behaviour varies over time and across situations and such behaviour can be said to exist on a continuum rather than being dichotomous. For example a young person may be extremely extraverted when with friends but rather introverted when with parents. Extraversion-introversion exists in terms of dimensions rather than in two discrete categories. Similarly, behaviour considered abnormal can also be said to exist on a continuum. For example, in the U.K. about three million people hear voices and many of these will never have contact with psychiatrists (Morrison, 2004).

Many psychological theorists such as Freud, Rogers, and Maslow regarded psychopathology as a difference in degree rather than category (Ewen, 1993). Furthermore, personality theorists challenged the assumption that there is a clear dividing line between normal functioning and psychotic illness (Bentall, 2004). Rather, they argue that psychopathology exists on a health-illness continuum. Empirical evidence supports this view, for example borderline personality disorder was found to exist on a continuum rather than as a dichotomy (Shevlin et al., 2007). The dimensional model can be viewed as a positive outcome for patients since a belief in the discrete model can result in the view that patients diagnosed with mental illness are categorically different from the rest of humanity (Read & Haslam, 2004). Mental health is a matter of degree and dimensional measures of mental health are more reliable than diagnoses (Read, 2004d). A dimensional, as opposed to a categorical, approach to mental health produces descriptions of people engaging in certain behaviours or thoughts to various degrees and depending to a large extent on what is happening in their immediate environments (Read, 2004d). Schizophrenia has blurred borders not only with normal behaviour but also with other mental health conditions such as bipolar disorder and depression. This is one reason why people may be given different diagnoses by different clinicians (The Schizophrenia Commission, 2012).

Within psychology there are many dimensional measures of constructs that relate to mental health, and schizotypy is one such construct. The term schizotypy is used to describe a diverse range of characteristics symptomatic of schizotypal personality disorder and refers to traits that are similar to symptoms of schizophrenia (Kerns, 2006; Rawlings, Claridge & Freeman, 2001). Schizotypy is a multidimensional personality trait that varies along a health-illness continuum (Fonseca-Pedrero, Lemos-Giraldez et al., 2008). At the illness end of the schizotypy spectrum lies schizotypal personality disorder. Schizotypal personality disorder is characterized by: a discomfort with, and a reduced capacity for close relationships; cognitive or perceptual distortions; and eccentricities of behaviour. Individuals suffering from schizotypal personality disorder may be overly superstitious, preoccupied with paranormal phenomena, may believe they have special psychic powers, may think they have magical control over others, and may sense the presence of someone when no one is there. Schizotypal personality disorder has been reported to occur in about 3% of the general population (APA, 2000; DSM-IV-TR).

There is evidence that schizotypal personality disorder may be very closely related to schizophrenia. Specifically, schizotypal personality disorder is more common in individuals who have biological relatives with schizophrenia, some of the symptoms of schizotypal personality disorder can be successfully treated with drugs used to treat schizophrenia, and many of the attentional and working memory deficits found in schizophrenia are also apparent in schizotypal personality disorder (Davey, 2008).

Since schizotypal personality disorder may represent a risk factor for schizophrenia (Davey, 2008), measuring schizotypy can facilitate the identification of people at risk for schizophrenia-spectrum disorders. Schizotypy, also known as psychosis-proneness, signifies the hereditary predisposition to schizophrenia (Claridge, 1997). Although the majority of schizotypal subjects will never develop the clinical form of psychosis it is possible that they share a common vulnerability with schizophrenic patients (Fonseca-Pedora, Paino et al., 2008).

Research with schizophrenic patients has found that the symptoms of schizophrenia group into three independent clusters: positive symptoms (hallucinations and delusions), negative symptoms (introversion and inability to experience pleasurable emotions), and symptoms of cognitive disorganisation. Research on measures of schizotypy found that they reflected the same three clusters identified by schizophrenia researchers (Bentall, 2004; Kerns, 2006). In both schizophrenia and schizotypy research females present higher levels of positive symptoms while males present higher levels of negative symptoms (Davey, 2008; Fonseca-Pedrero, Lemos-Giraldez et al., 2008).

Giving consideration to the above schizotypy was used as a measure of predisposition to schizophrenia in this book.

Chapter 7

Measuring Schizotypy

This chapter looks at how schizotypy has been measured and describes the measure of schizotypy employed in this study.

Many self-report scales have been developed for measuring schizotypy in non-clinical samples. Despite the multiplicity of scales, a consensus seems to have established that schizotypy reduces to three components, 'positive schizotypy', 'cognitive disorganisation' and 'negative schizotypy' (Mason & Claridge, 2006). With this in mind the 104-item Oxford-Liverpool Inventory of Feelings and Experiences (O-Life) was developed by Mason et al. (1995). The O-Life items are based on the most extensive study of schizotypal traits undertaken. The results of this study revealed that as well as the three aforementioned components, a fourth component emerged namely 'asocial behaviour' (Mason & Claridge, 2006). The O-Life scale incorporates these four components. The scale comprises four subscales: Unusual Experiences (UnEx: measuring positive schizotypy); Cognitive Disorganisation (CogDis); Introvertive Anhedonia (InAn: measuring negative schizotypy); and Impulsive Nonconformity (ImpCon: measuring asocial behaviour).

Symptoms of positive schizotypy (UnEx) include perceptual aberrations, magical thinking, and hallucinations. Symptoms of cognitive disorganisation (CogDis) include poor attention and concentration, poor decision making, thought disorder, and social anxiety. Symptoms of negative schizotypy (InAn) include lack of enjoyment from social and physical sources of pleasure, and an avoidance of intimacy. Symptoms of impulsive nonconformity (ImpCon) include impulsive, antisocial and eccentric forms of behaviour suggesting a lack of self-control (Mason, Linney, & Claridge, 2005).

The items from the O-Life scale correspond to the DSM-IV-TR diagnostic criteria for Schizotypal Personality Disorder. The O-Life scale has been shown to be valid since many studies have shown that high scorers in schizotypy show similar neurocognitive deficits to those found in schizophrenic patients (Batey & Furnham, 2008). Since the O-Life scale may be excessively long for some studies a short version (O-Life SF: 43-items) was developed by Mason et al. (2005). The O-Life SF demonstrated satisfactory levels of reliability and validity (Mason et al., 2005). The O-Life SF was employed to measure schizotypy in this study.

All subscales of the O-Life SF are scored on 'yes' (1), 'no' (0) format. The UnEx subscale comprises 12 items with a possible response range of 0-12. Sample items from the

UnEx subscale include, 'When in the dark do you often see shapes and forms even though there is nothing there?' and 'do you think that you could learn to read other's minds if you wanted to?' The CogDis subscale comprises 11 items with a possible response range of 0-11. Sample items from the CogDis subscale include, 'Are you easily distracted from work by daydreams?' and 'when in a crowded room, do you often have difficulty in following a conversation?' The InAn subscale comprises 10 items with a possible response range of 0-10. Sample items from the InAn subscale include, 'Are there very few things that you have ever enjoyed doing?' and 'Do you feel very close to your friends? The ImpCon subscale comprises 10 items with a possible response range of 0-10. Sample items from the ImpCon subscale include, 'Would you like other people to be afraid of you?' and 'Do you often feel like doing the opposite of what other people suggest even though you know they are right?'

Chapter 8

Measuring Religion

This chapter looks at how religion is measured, examines the differences between religion and spirituality, and describes how religion is measured in this study.

Within psychology and sociological disciplines being religious is often referred to by the term religiosity. Religiosity can be understood in terms of the degree to which a person is religious or the extent to which they practice their religion through overt or covert behaviour. Religiosity is most often measured in terms of church attendance, frequency of prayer, study of religious texts and relationship with Jesus and/or God.

Recently there has been a tendency to substitute the word spiritual for religious, particularly when individuals are describing experiences that they do not wish to associate with dogmatic belief systems (Corbett, 1996). Furthermore, a growing disillusionment with religious institutions has resulted in spirituality acquiring distinct meanings and connotations separate from religion (Hill & Hood, 1999).

Spirituality may refer to a subjective experience of the sacred while religion involves a subscription to a set of institutionalized beliefs (Holder et al., 2000). Spirituality is more comprehensive than religion but includes religion

(Hull, 2002). Many now believe that they do not need institutions or priests telling them how to live their lives, rather they rely on guidance from the spirit within. The important feature of spirituality is not a sense of duty to the church but a responsibility to find the true self within. For some, being spiritual simply amounts to accepting that there is a mystery context to existence with no real need to understand, talk to, worship, adore or fear it (O'Doherty, 2008).

The word religion comes from a Latin root *religio* which signifies a bond between humanity and some 'greater than human power', while the word spirituality comes from a Latin root *spiritus,* meaning breath of life (Hill et al., 2000). Despite conceptual differences religion and spirituality share many common characteristics (Hill et al., 2000) and in empirical terms the differences may be slight. For example, James (1985) suggested that religion consisted of the belief that there is an unseen order and that our supreme good lies in harmoniously adjusting ourselves to this supreme good. Arguably, James' definition applies equally to spirituality as well as religion. Jung (1938) defined religion as the careful and scrupulous observation of the numinosum (divine manifestations). Spirituality could be similarly defined. Furthermore, Zohar and Marshall (2000) propose that to experience the spiritual means to be in touch with some larger, deeper, richer whole that puts the present situation into a new perspective. Arguably, religious experience could be defined in similar terms, and the terms religious experience and spiritual experience are often used interchangeably. Spirituality might be what all religious-cultural traditions have in common (Loewenthal, 2000), and it has been a core conception of religion for thousands of years (Hood et al., 1996). Marler and Hadaway (2002) conclude that the most 'spiritual', by a variety of measures, are those who are the most 'religious'.

Although there is some disagreement about what is meant by the terms religion and spirituality, many agree that prayer is the most salient measure of religiosity since it taps into the more spiritual dimensions of religion (cf. Breslin & Lewis, 2008) as opposed to the more organisational, institutional, and dogmatic aspects. It has been argued that prayer should be measured using a multi-item scale that takes account of different thoughts during prayer (Ladd & Spilka, 2002), and recognises the different types of prayer such as petitionary prayer and meditative prayer (Poloma & Pendleton, 1991). However, Breslin and Lewis (2013) found that a multi-item measure of prayer had little utility over and above a single item frequency of prayer measure. In this study religiosity was measured using a frequency of prayer measure, a frequency of church attendance measure, and a frequency of reading the Bible (or other religious text) measure.

Response options for the three religiosity measures ranged from 'never' (1), through 'at least weekly' (4), to 'several times a day' (7). The three items were summed to yield a measure of Total Religiosity with a possible response range of 3-21.

Chapter 9
Relationship between Schizotypy and Religion

There has been little research on the relationship between schizotypy and religiosity in Ireland. However, there has been a considerable body of research on schizotypy and religiosity generally. Some of this research was concerned with religious orientation and schizotypy while the remainder was concerned with religiosity in general.

Religious orientation is concerned with how people practice their religion, specifically, whether people see religion as an end in itself (intrinsic orientation) or a means to an end (extrinsic orientation). For example, a person with high levels of extrinsic religious orientation might attend religious services to meet people or to be seen, whereas a person with high levels of intrinsic religious orientation might attend religious services to feel closer to the Divine. Studies concerned with religious orientation reported: 1) an intrinsic orientation towards religion is associated with lower levels of schizotypy while an extrinsic orientation towards religion is associated with higher levels of schizotypy (Maltby & Day, 2002); 2) schizotypal traits did not predict either intrinsic or extrinsic religious orientation (Joseph, Smith, & Diduca, 2002); and 3) an intrinsic orientation was associated with lower levels of borderline personality disorder among men, while an extrinsic orientation was associated with higher levels of borderline personality disorder among women (Maltby et al., 2000). Taken together, these studies provide little evidence for a clear relationship between schizotypy and religious orientation.

Other studies reported: 1) a positive association between religiosity and magical ideation for boys but not for girls and a positive association between religiosity and impulsive nonconformity for girls but not for boys (ages 13-18) (Joseph & Diduca, 2001); 2) a positive association between religious preoccupation and magical ideation in males but not females (Diduca & Joseph, 1997); and 3) a positive association between religiosity and unusual perceptual experiences in males but not females (White, Joseph, & Neil, 1995).

Research on members of new religious movements (NRM) found that they scored significantly higher on measures of schizotypy than both non-religious and religious control groups. Furthermore, there was no significant difference in scores on a schizotypy measure between NRM members and a control group suffering from delusions. However, no significant difference in schizotypy scores was found between the non-religious and religious groups. (Day & Peters, 1999; Peters, Day, McKenna, & Orbach, 1999). Mohr and Huguelet (2004) reported that spirituality was used to a large extent to cope with schizophrenia among outpatients. However, they found that spiritual and religious concerns were just as likely to add to patients' problems as help them to cope with problems.

Low-schizotypy individuals were more likely to view God as a person, view religion as being a rational choice and being central to their lives, and more likely to accept religion without question. Conversely, high-schizotypy individuals were more likely to view God as a supernatural power, view religion as being less of a rational choice and less central to their lives, and less likely to accept religion without question (Tiliopoulos & Bikker, 2013).

Schizotypy was negatively related to frequency of prayer but positively related to temple attendance (Lesmana & Tiliopoulos, 2009). There was a significant positive association between spiritual experiences and schizotypy among both a normal sample and a clinical sample. However, the clinical sample had significantly more spiritual experiences than the normal sample, and scored significantly higher on the schizotypy scale than the normal sample (Jackson, 1997). Unterrainer et al. (2011) reported that magical thinking was significantly positively associated with religious and spiritual well-being. However, they pointed out that dimensions of religious and spiritual well-being might be either indicative of a creative or a disordered personality.

Prayer was positively associated with magical ideation and unusual experiences, among an Irish sample (Breslin & Lewis, under review). Prayer fulfilment (an experience of joy that results from prayer) and religious crisis (feelings of alienation and abandonment by God) were positively associated with schizotypal personality disorder (Piedmont, 2009).

Taken together the above studies suggest a gender specific, weak positive association between religiosity and schizotypy.

Other Measures employed in the study

In addition to schizotypy and religiosity measures, respondents were also asked about their perceived level of happiness, their perceived level of physical health, their perceived level of mental health, and their level of alcohol consumption. Happiness was measured by the item 'On average, over the past six months how happy have you been?' Response options ranged from 'very unhappy' (1), through 'slightly happy' (4), to 'very happy' (6). Physical health was measured by the item 'On average, over the past six months how ***physically*** healthy have you been?' Response options ranged from 'very unhealthy' (1), through 'slightly healthy' (4), to 'very healthy' (6). Mental health was measured by the item 'On average, over the past six months how *mentally* healthy have you been?' Response options ranged from 'very unhealthy' (1), through 'slightly healthy' (4), to 'very healthy' (6). Alcohol consumption was measured by the item 'On average, how many units of alcohol do you drink per day?' The concept of a unit of alcohol was explained and response options included even numbers only in the range from 0-20.

Although this book is concerned with the relationship between religion and mental health, physical health was also measured because physical health is associated with mental health in many different ways, for example, psychological problems can increase vulnerability to physical disease and physical disease can result in psychological symptoms (Kogan, Edelstein, & McKee, 2000). People with severe mental illness such as schizophrenia have poorer diets, take less exercise and smoke more than the general population (The Schizophrenia Commission, 2012). Furthermore, physical health status has been shown to be related to psychological well-being (Whelan, 1994). Additionally, the onset of health problems can often lead to depression, anxiety and other psychiatric disorders. For example, pain and depression often reinforce each other and level of disability is one of the strongest predictors of depression in medical patients (Koenig, 2009).

Relationship between Schizotypy and Religion

Respondents were also asked to state the country in which they grew up and what their religious denomination was.

Chapter 10

Methodology

This chapter describes the methodology employed in the study and explains, for the interested reader, the statistical analyses employed in the results section.

Respondents comprised an opportunistic sample of 385 who completed the online questionnaire (survey methodology). Respondents were recruited by friends and acquaintances of the researchers who were asked to complete the questionnaire and were requested to ask their friends and acquaintances to complete it who in turn asked their friends and acquaintances to complete it.

Respondents were from Ireland (N = 135), U.S.A. (N = 142), U.K. (N = 32), Canada (N = 24), Northern Ireland (N=5). The remainder (N = 47) were from 24 different countries. The mean age of respondents was 33.18 (SD = 12.57). The sex distribution was 43.9% female and 56.1% male.

Respondents' religious denomination included Catholic (N = 116), Atheist (N = 115), Protestant (N = 40), Agnostic (N = 39), Buddhist (N =14), Pagan (N =10), Jewish (N =8), Muslim (N =5), Bahai (N =5), Hindu (N =2), Sikh (N =1), other religion (N =30).

Methodology

Understanding the statistics

The discipline of statistics has been called the most important science of them all by Florence Nightingale. On the other hand a famous quote often attributed to Benjamin Disraeli states that 'there are three kinds of lies: lies, damn lies and statistics'. Whatever your view there is no doubt that statistics are a very important tool in many scientific disciplines including psychology and medicine. This short section is designed to explain the statistics used in analysing the data in this study, the results of which are reported in the next two chapters.

One function of statistics is to indicate when the different scores on variable A (in this case, mental health) between two groups of people are due to the effect of another variable B (in this case, religion) and when it is simply due to chance. Even if there is no effect from B, the mean (average) scores of the two groups are highly unlikely to be the same. Within psychological research the probability of the difference being due to chance is usually set at 95%. If the difference in scores is so big that there is only a 5% probability that it was due to chance, then the researcher generally accepts that the difference was due to B. The findings are then said to be statistically significant and $P<.05$ denotes that the probability that the findings were due to chance is less than 5%.

Statistical tests are often described as one-tailed or two-tailed, describing whether they examine a one test scenario or a more complex one. If we wanted to test one thing, for example whether religious people had better levels of mental health than atheists, we would use a one-tailed test but if we wanted to explore if religious people and atheists had different levels (could be either better or worse) of mental health we would use a two-tailed test. It is more difficult to find an effect using a two-tailed test because the 95% probability of chance is split between the two levels - better and worse levels of mental health, similarly the 5% probability for the effect of religion is split between the two levels. For example, with a two-tailed test a finding that religious people had better mental health than atheists requires that the difference in scores between the two groups would need to be so big that there is only a 2.5% probability of finding this difference if it was due to chance. So we take it that the difference is due to religion. The statistical tests used in the results section are all two-tailed.

A t test compares the average or mean score of two groups but it also takes into consideration the spread of the scores within the groups. The spread of scores around the mean is measured by the standard deviation (SD). Although the difference between the mean scores of two groups may not look that big, the difference may still be statistically significant because the spread of the scores within the groups is relatively small. In other words the result of a t test is a function of the spread of the scores within the groups as well as the difference in means between groups.

A correlation index examines the linear relationship between two variables, i.e. how two variables change together. The index has an absolute value ranging from 0 to 1 and can be either positive or negative. If two variables change together (or co-vary) this implies that they are related but not necessarily causally related, they may or may not be causally related. For example, a third variable could be causing the change.

Within psychology a number of questionnaire items are sometimes used to measure a particular construct. For example a three item scale was used in this study to measure religiosity, namely frequency of prayer, church attendance and Bible reading. A scale in psychology needs to produce scores that are reliable in the same way that a measure in the physical world needs to produce measurements that are reliable, for example a tape measure gives a reliable measurement each time it is used. In a good scale each item should measure the same thing, for example each of the three items should measure an aspect of religiosity. If each item measures the same thing then each item should correlate with each other. For example frequency of prayer should correlate with the other two items in the scale. Within psychology there is a statistical test for the reliability of the scores from a scale and it yields a statistical index called Cronbach's alpha. Cronbach's alpha is similar to the average correlation between all the items in a scale. An alpha value of .7 or above is generally regarded as indicative of a reliable scale.

Chapter 11

Relationship between Religion and Mental Health

This chapter reports the findings of the study in relation to measures of schizotypy, mental health, happiness, and physical health and discusses the implications of these findings.

As can be seen from Table 1 (page 69) estimates of reliability for the Religiosity, Unusual Experiences, and Cognitive Disorganisation scales were satisfactory, with the level of Cronbach's alpha (Cronbach 1951) being greater than .7 (Kline, 1986). However, estimates of reliability for the Introvertive Anhedonia and Impulsive Nonconformity were less than satisfactory. Table 1 also shows the means and standard deviations for the measures. The means and standard deviations shown in Table 1 suggest that overall the sample were not very religious, engaging in religious activities, on average, about once a month. Even when atheists were excluded from the analysis the scores on Religiosity only increased by 1.26, a small increase on a scale ranging from 3 to 21.

Table 1 also indicates that respondents were more happy than unhappy, more physically healthy than unhealthy, and more mentally healthy than unhealthy since the average scores indicated that the respondents were somewhere between slightly happy and happy and somewhere between slightly healthy and healthy both mentally and physically.

The average alcohol consumption was 1.39 units (standard drinks) per day, the equivalent of a medium sized glass of wine or a bottle of strong beer. This is equivalent to 9.7 standard drinks per week. The average alcohol consumption for respondents who grew up in Ireland was 17.5 standard drinks per week for males and 14.2 standard drinks for females. Overall, the rate of alcohol consumption was moderate and well within the healthy drinking guidelines, which are 11 and 17 standard drinks per week for females and males respectively (Hope, 2009). However, for Irish females the rate of alcohol consumption was considerably higher than the healthy drinking guidelines (14.2 vs. 11). This higher rate reflects the fact that a binge drinking culture among Irish women has become more socially acceptable. Despite this, men continue to drink more and to suffer more alcohol-related health problems than women (Mongon et al., 2007). Generally in Ireland the amount of alcohol consumed is 21 standard drinks for every adult aged 15 years and older. This is equivalent to 51 bottles of vodka per year (Hope, 2009). This is much higher than the consumption rates of Irish respondents within the present sample.

In terms of the schizotypy measures Table 1 shows that respondents scored highest on Cognitive Disorganisation.

Table 1. Alpha, means and standard deviations for all measures.

Measures	Alpha	Mean	SD
Total Religiosity	.77	6.95	4.36
Happiness	-	4.31	1.31
Physical Health	-	4.39	1.16
Mental Health	-	4.58	1.22
Alcohol Consumption	-	1.39	2.21
Unusual Experiences	.73	2.74	2.46
Cognitive Disorganisation	.77	3.99	2.84
Introvertive Anhedonia	.61	2.43	2.00
Impulsive Nonconformity	.57	2.67	1.96

Since one aim of the study was to examine the effects of religion on mental health, Catholics and atheists were compared on the measures shown in Table 2 (page 71). Table 2 shows that although atheists had higher levels of happiness, better physical health, and better mental health only the difference in mental health was statistically significant. This lends support to Dawkins' (2006) contention that atheists can lead happy and fulfilled lives without religion. The results do not corroborate MacLachlan and Hand's (2013) findings that religion had a small positive influence on happiness on Irish respondents. Table 2 also shows that Catholics had more unusual experiences and experienced more cognitive disorganisation than atheists and these differences were statistically significant. Since unusual experiences is one of the facets of schizotypy which best predicts future psychosis (Hewitt & Claridge, 1989), our findings lend some support to Scheper-Hughes' contention that there may be a relationship between religion, specifically Catholicism, and schizophrenia.

Table 2. Means and standard deviations of the measures for Catholics and atheists

Measures	Catholics	Atheists
Happiness[a]	4.17 (1.30)	4.36 (1.33)
Physical Health[b]	4.19 (1.13)	4.46(1.11)
Mental Health[c]	4.45 (1.14)	4.78 (1.26)
UnEx[d]	3.02 (2.65)	2.03 (1.99)
CogDis[e]	4.64 (3.02)	3.76 (2.78)
InAn[f]	2.31 (1.83)	2.49 (2.15)
ImpCon[g]	2.64 (1.95)	2.67 (1.86)

Key
a $t(229) = -1.06, p>.05$
b $t(229) = -1.84, p>.05$
c $t(229) = -2.12, p<.05$
d $t(213) = 3.19, p<.05$
e $t(229) = 2.28, p<.05$
f $t(229) = -0.67, p>.05$
g $t(229) = -0.13, p>.05$

A further aim of the study was to examine the differences between Irish respondents and U.S.A. respondents on the mental health variables. Table 3 (page 72) shows that although U.S.A. respondents had higher levels of happiness, better physical health, and better mental health, only the difference in mental health was statistically significant. Furthermore, Table 3 shows that Irish respondents had more unusual experiences and experienced more cognitive disorganisation than U.S.A. respondents and these differences were statistically significant. These findings lend some support to Scheper-Hughes' contention that the Irish may be more predisposed to schizophrenia than other ethnic groups.

Table 3. Means and standard deviations of the measures for Irish and U.S.A. respondents.

Measures	Irish	U.S.A.
Happiness[a]	4.19 (1.36)	4.34 (1.30)
Physical Health[b]	4.22 (1.16)	4.49(1.15)
Mental Health[c]	4.38 (1.23)	4.63 (1.28)
UnEx[d]	3.08 (2.67)	2.46 (2.06)
CogDis[e]	5.00 (3.01)	3.60 (2.69)
InAn[f]	2.37 (1.81)	2.39 (2.16)
ImpCon[g]	2.78 (2.04)	2.70 (1.97)

Key

a	$t(275) = -0.96, p > .05$
b	$t(275) = -1.90, p > .05$
c	$t(275) = -1.70, p < .05$
d	$t(252) = 2.15, p < .05$
e	$t(268) = 2.62, p < .05$
f	$t(275) = -0.10, p > .05$
g	$t(275) = 0.33, p > .05$

To give consideration to Scheper-Hughes' suggestion that poor mental health is disguised under the cloak of alcohol the correlations between alcohol consumption, religiosity, and the mental health variables were examined. If poor mental health is disguised under the cloak of alcohol then there are two possible scenarios. Firstly, it might be expected that as alcohol consumption increases mental health and happiness improves, i.e. there is a linear relationship. Secondly, it is possible that as alcohol consumption increases mental health and happiness improves initially but as consumption continues to increase mental health and happiness begins to decrease, i.e. there is a curvilinear relationship. Both of these scenarios were examined and it was found that there were no curvilinear relationships between alcohol consumption and any of the variables presented in Table 4 (page 75). Table 4 shows the correlations, which are a measure of the linear relationships. The only statistically significant correlations were for religiosity, physical health and Impulsive Nonconformity. For religiosity the negative correlation suggests that the more religious a person is the less they drink. This corroborates previous research which reported significantly lower alcohol use, abuse and addiction in people who were more religious (Koenig, 2009). For physical health the negative correlation suggests that the more a person drinks the worse their physical health will be. For Impulsive Nonconformity the positive correlation suggests that the more a person drinks the more they are inclined to be non-conforming and impulsive. When the correlations were calculated again among respondents who grew up in Ireland only, a similar pattern of correlations emerged, the only difference being that the correlation between alcohol consumption and physical health was not statistically significant. The general lack of significant correlations between mental health and alcohol consumption, and happiness and alcohol consumption suggests that poor mental health is not disguised under the cloak of alcohol, lending no support to Scheper-Hughes' suggestion. Despite this, it could be argued there was no correlation between mental health and alcohol because the people who drink do so in order to bring their level of mental health on a par with non-drinkers thus masking any effect for alcohol within the sample. To control for this, only drinkers were selected from the sample and the correlations between alcohol consumption and mental health and alcohol consumption and happiness were calculated again. As before there were no significant correlations between these variables among drinkers, suggesting that poor mental health is not disguised under the cloak of alcohol.

Table 4. Correlations between alcohol consumption and the measures.

Measure	Alcohol	p value (two tailed)
Religiosity	-.16	*P*<.01
Happiness	.00	*p*>.05
Physical Health	-.11	*P*<.05
Mental Health	-.04	*p*>.05
Unusual Experiences	.08	*p*>.05
Cognitive Disorganisation	.09	*p*>.05
Introvertive Anhedonia	-.07	*p*>.05
Impulsive Nonconformity	.16	*P*<.01

To sum up the findings reported in this chapter, atheists had significantly better mental health than Catholics. In terms of schizotypy, Catholics had significantly more unusual experiences and experienced significantly more cognitive disorganisation than atheists. U.S.A. respondents had significantly better mental health than Irish respondents. Again, in terms of schizotypy, Irish respondents had significantly more unusual experiences and experienced significantly more cognitive disorganisation than U.S.A. respondents. Alcohol consumption was significantly negatively related to physical health and significantly positively related to Impulsive Nonconformity. These results are discussed further in chapter 13.

Chapter 12

Religious Practice in Ireland

This chapter reports the findings of the study in relation to the prevalence of religious practice in Ireland and discusses the implications of these findings.

Among the respondents who grew up in Ireland in the present study 63% were Catholic, 4.4% were Protestant and 17.8% were atheist. In Census 2011 the breakdown by religious denomination of people born in Ireland indicated that 89.8% were Catholic, 3.5% were Protestant and 4.4% had no religion (CSO, 2012a). A similar breakdown from Census 1971, the closest census to when Scheper-Hughes conducted her research, indicated that 93.9% were Catholic, 4.0% were Protestant and 0.3% had no religion (CSO, 2012b). The increase in the number of people with no religion is substantial and is reflective of the fact that the rate of religious decline is faster than anywhere else in Europe (O'Doherty, 2008). In the present study 17.8% were atheist which is considerably higher than the percentage who described themselves as having no religion in Census 2011. However, the census form did not offer the option of atheist and some atheists who were born Catholic may have chosen the latter option instead of no religion.

Nic Ghiolla Phádraig (2009) traced religious change over time in the Republic of Ireland and reported that almost all respondents who were raised as Catholics still claim this affiliation. She reported that 16% of self-declared Catholics were atheist, agnostic or did not believe in a personal God. She also reported that, among Irish Catholics, attendance at a religious service at least once a week declined from 90% in 1973 to 43% in 2008, and this pattern was mirrored by other religious denominations. In the present study 21% of respondents who grew up in Ireland attended a religious service at least once a week. She also reported a decline in frequency of prayer with over 70% of respondents praying several times a week in 1991 and less than 50% praying several times a week in 2008. In the present study 26% of respondents who grew up in Ireland prayed several times a week, while 17% prayed at least weekly.

A number of reasons have been proposed to explain the decline in religiosity, including economic growth. It has been argued that religion compensates for existential insecurity and, from an economic perspective, the demand for religious 'products' decreases with economic prosperity. Religion compensates for economic and physical insecurity therefore as economic security increases the need for religion diminishes. Individuals raised in a more secure economic climate tend to develop values that are less compatible with traditional religion (Hirschle, 2009).

Another perception is that economic development leads to more engagement with consumer-related activities. Many consumer-related activities are designed to disconnect people from the reality of their everyday lives and to help them cope with the mundaneness of life. This function is served by bars, discos, video games and theme parks, for example. The activities associated with the consumer society are competing with the sense of meaning and social cohesion that were once provided by traditional religion. With economic development an increase in purchasing power presents consumption opportunities that compete with traditional religion leading to a decline in religiosity (Hirschle, 2009).

Hirschle (2009) investigated the relationship between economic growth and religious attendance in Ireland between 1988 until 2005. During this period Gross Domestic Product (GDP) and household income steadily increased. He found that a strong religious decline accompanied economic development particularly among the youngest cohorts. Specifically, net household income negatively predicted church attendance. Furthermore, net household income was the strongest predictor of church attendance even after controlling for educational level, employment status, hours spent at work, and urban/rural context. Hirschle concluded that these findings provide some support for the consumption-related explanation for religious decline. Since consumption generally increases with household wealth, perhaps these findings provide support for the biblical contention that it is much harder for a rich person to enter the Kingdom of God than for a camel to go through the eye of a needle (Matthew 19:24).

O'Doherty (2008), in his book Empty Pulpits, gives little consideration to consumption as a reason for religious decline in Ireland, pointing out that atheists and believers were united by the consumer society. Rather, the decline began after Vatican II when peoples' hopes and aspirations were initially raised by the expectation of a reformed and more open church only to be dashed by the subsequent papal ruling on contraception. The ruling on contraception showed that the church wasn't listening to the people and consequently the people began to stop listening to the church. O'Doherty argued that the church's teaching on sex resulted in a dramatic reduction of the influence of the hierarchy on the people, particularly teenagers and young adults. Subsequently when the sex abuse scandals emerged, the tenuous moral authority of the church could not survive the dichotomy between what the church preached and what it practised. Many Catholics turned away from the religious authority of the church, which was prescribing how they lived their lives. According to O'Doherty, the Catholics that remained with the church were a la carte Catholics and would be more aptly named Protestant since they did not agree with many of the teachings of the Catholic church.

O'Doherty suggested further explanations for religious decline as follows. In Ireland religion was predominantly a social activity and the mass acted as a mechanism for bonding the community. If you did not attend mass your absence would be noted. Before the age of computers, multimedia, sports bars, sports clubs and leisure centres people had less activity in their lives and had more time for community bonding. As people pursued other activities, they may have used these activities as occasions for community bonding or they may have had less time for or less interest in community bonding and the habit of going to mass declined. Consequently, the reduction of church attendance could be seen more as a disruption of tradition than as a collapse in faith.

Urbanization led to a reduction in church attendance because there was no longer a pressure to conform to rural customs and people no longer felt scrutinized by their neighbours and judged for non-attendance. When Irish people moved to big cities like London and Liverpool their religious attendance declined, suggesting that they were attending church because of a social need rather than spiritual one, or alternatively, moving to the big city met the spiritual need (O'Doherty, 2008).

It is likely that all of the above explanations contributed to the decline of religious practice in Ireland and the results of the present study suggest that this decline is set to continue.

Chapter 13

Conclusion

This book set out to examine the prevalence of religious practice in Ireland, to examine the relationship between religion and mental health, and to ascertain if there was any relationship between religion, specifically Catholicism, and schizophrenia as suggested by Scheper-Hughes. Another aim was to compare the mental health of Irish respondents with U.S.A. respondents with a view to examining Scheper-Hughes' (2001) claim that the Irish had psychiatric rates that far exceeded other ethnic groups. A further aim was to investigate the relationship between alcohol and mental health variables with a view to examining Scheper-Hughes' (2001) claim that a certain level of mental illness is tolerated in Ireland when it is disguised under the cloak of alcohol.

As discussed in Chapter 12 it seems that the present decline in religious practice in Ireland is likely to continue. However, this is unlikely to have a negative impact on mental health since the study found that atheists had significantly better mental health than Catholics. Although Catholics would undoubtedly engage in religious duties more so than atheists it may not be religious duties but rather religious experience which is beneficial to mental health. Wilson (2009) suggested that a transcendental experience with God is one of the primary effectors of change among people with mental health problems. Corbett (1996) argued that religion has become de-spiritualized while Keane (2009) pointed out that although most people adopted a more spiritual outlook on life after a near death experience they were not necessarily more committed to performing religious duties, suggesting that religious duties and religious experience are not necessarily related. James (1985) contended that the fountainhead of all religions lies in the mystical experience of the individual. In the present sample it may be that atheists had more mystical experiences then religious people since atheists had significantly better mental health. Religious or mystical experiences may be few and far between in the population, as suggested by Breslin and Lewis (2010) who reported that respondents rarely had such experiences. Further research could explore the relationship between religious experience and mental health. However, the difficulty is likely to be in finding a big enough sample of respondents who have had a religious experience.

The study found support for a relationship between religion, specifically Catholicism, and schizophrenia as suggested by Scheper-Hughes (2001) to the extent that Catholics had significantly higher scores than atheists in two out of the four schizotypy subscales i.e., Unusual Experiences and Cognitive Disorganisation. Unfortunately, there were not enough respondents to test if Irish Catholics had higher scores than Catholics of other nations. If they did this would suggest an ethnic predisposition to schizophrenia as opposed to a religious predisposition. Future research could address this issue.

In terms of an ethnic predisposition to schizophrenia the study lends support to Scheper-Hughes' suggestion that the Irish may be more predisposed to mental health problems than other ethnic groups. Specifically, U.S.A. respondents had significantly better mental health than Irish respondents and Irish respondents were significantly more predisposed to schizophrenia than U.S.A. respondents as reflected in the fact that Irish respondents had significantly higher scores than U.S.A. respondents in two out of the four schizotypy subscales i.e., Unusual Experiences and Cognitive Disorganisation. Future research could compare Irish respondents with other ethnic groups to ascertain if the Irish are more predisposed to mental health problems than other ethnic groups apart from U.S.A. respondents.

As well as indicative of predisposition to schizophrenia, schizotypy is positively related to creative thinking (Folley & Park, 2005) and may play a role in determining creative pursuits, for example in one study creative arts students scored higher on the unusual experiences dimension of schizotypy compared to humanities students (O'Reilly et al., 2001). Higher levels of unusual experiences are generally associated with higher levels of creativity (Batey & Furnham, 2008). Visual artists have higher levels of unusual experiences than non-artists (Burch et al., 2006), and some poets and artists have levels of unusual experiences that can be as high as schizophrenia patients (Nettle, 2006). The above research in conjunction with the present findings suggest that the Irish are a creative people and anecdotally this is perceived to be the case. Perhaps Scheper-Hughes was alluding to this creativity when she declared that the saints, scholars and schizophrenics of Ireland were all culture bearers of the same tradition.

Although alcohol consumption was positively related to Impulsive Nonconformity and negatively related to physical health the findings of this study suggest that poor mental health is not disguised under the cloak of alcohol in Ireland as proposed by Scheper-Hughes. However, it has to be borne in mind that generally the rate of alcohol consumption among respondents in this study was moderate and well within the healthy drinking guidelines. It may be that if the respondents had been heavier drinkers then a negative relationship between alcohol and mental health would have emerged. Future research among a sample of heavier drinkers could examine this hypothesis.

In terms of drink and religion there was a significant negative relationship between alcohol consumption and religiosity suggesting that the more religious a person is the less they drink. This may help explain why alcoholics anonymous (AA) believe that spirituality is essential for recovery from alcoholism. The key to success of organisations such as AA include: the admission by the person that they do not have the power to overcome their problem alone, the decision to surrender to a higher power, and the commitment to help others with their alcohol addiction (Koenig, 2009).

Jung argued that a craving for alcohol was analogous to a spiritual thirst for wholeness or union with God. He pointed out that the word for alcohol in Latin is 'spiritus' and this same word is used for the highest religious experience (Kurtz & Ketcham, 2002). Again it may be religious experience as opposed to performing religious duties which may be beneficial to mental health.

A limitation of the study was the small sample size and the fact that the sample was not randomly selected, making it difficult to generalize the findings to the rest of the population. The fact that than an online survey was employed may have precluded certain sections of the population particularly those who were not computer literate. The online survey may also have resulted in a younger cohort of

Conclusion

respondents, as reflected by the average age of respondents being 33. Older respondents may have produced a different result particularly since religiosity tends to increase with age (Argue, Johnson, & White, 1999) and bearing in mind that the sample in this study were not very religious as reflected in the mean score on the Religiosity measure. Another limitation is that it was not possible to examine which was the best predictor of predisposition to schizophrenia, being Irish, being Catholic, or being both Irish and Catholic. A further limitation was the lack of other ethnic groups, apart from U.S.A. respondents, to compare Irish respondents with in terms of predisposition to schizophrenia. An additional limitation was the possibility that some of the findings were due to chance because of the number of statistical tests conducted. As outlined in chapter 10 the norm within psychology is to accept the result as valid if there is only a five percent probability that the result was due to chance. Nevertheless, as more statistical tests are conducted the probability that the results are due to chance increases above five percent. However, since this was an exploratory study statistical correction for this anomaly was deliberately not applied.

To conclude, Nancy Scheper-Hughes, employing ethnographic methodology reported in 1979 that Irish people were vulnerable to schizophrenia and mental health problems and that religion, particularly Catholicism, was a contributory factor. Even though the prevalence of religious practice in Ireland has declined in the intervening period, results from the present study using survey methodology almost 35 years later lends some support to Scheper-Hughes' findings. Despite the limitations outlined above, it is hoped that this short book will contribute to the existing knowledge in the area of religion and mental health and will stimulate an interest in the field that will lead to further illumination of the relationship between these two controversial and fascinating subjects.

References

American Psychiatric Association (APA) (2000). *Diagnostic and statistical manual of mental disorders: DSM-IV-TR.* Washington DC: Author.

Argue, A., Johnson, D.R., & White, L.K. (1999). Age and religiosity: Evidence from a three-wave panel analysis. *Journal for the Scientific Study of Religion, 38,* 423-435.

Batey, M., & Furnham, A. (2008). The relationship between measures of creativity and schizotypy. *Personality and Individual Differences, 45,* 816-821.

Beatty, J. (1995). *Principles of behavioral neuroscience.* Madison, WI: Brown & Benchmark Publishers.

Bentall, R.P. (2004). Abandoning the concept of schizophrenia: The cognitive psychology of hallucinations and delusions. In J. Read, L.R. Mosher, & R.P. Bentall (Eds.) (2004), *Models of madness: Psychological, social and biological approaches to schizophrenia* (pp. 195-208). Hove: Routledge.

Bergan, A., & McConatha, J.T. (2000). Religiosity and life satisfaction. *Activities, Adaptation and Aging, 24,* 23-34.

Biggar, H., Forehand, R., Devine, D., Brody, G., Armistead, L., Morse, E., & Simon, P. (1999). Women who are HIV infected: The role of religious activity in psychosocial adjustment. *AIDS Care, 11,* 195-199.

Borras, L., & Huguelet, P. (2009). Explanatory models of mental illness and its treatment. In P. Huguelet & H.G. Koenig (Eds.) (2009), *Religion and Spirituality in Psychiatry,* (pp. 268-282). New York: Cambridge University Press.

Braam, A.W. (2009). Religion/spirituality and mood disorders. In P. Huguelet & H.G. Koenig (Eds.) (2009), *Religion and Spirituality in Psychiatry,* (pp. 97-113). New York: Cambridge University Press.

Breslin, M.J. (2006). *Religion and mental health: Theoretical and empirical models of the effects of prayer.* Unpublished doctoral dissertation, University of Ulster at Magee, Derry, Northern Ireland.

Breslin, M.J., & Lewis, C.A. (2008). Theoretical models of the nature of prayer and health: A review. *Mental Health, Religion and Culture, 11,* 9-21.

Breslin, M.J., & Lewis, C.A. (2010). A psychometric evaluation of Poloma and Pendelton's (1991) Measure of Prayer Experience. *Journal of Beliefs and Values, 31,* 93-96.

References

Breslin, M.J., & Lewis, C.A. (2013). Eysenck's model of personality and prayer: The utility of a multidimensional approach. *Mental Health, Religion & Culture,* DOI:10.1080/13674676.2013.798721.

Breslin, M.J., & Lewis, C.A. (under review). Schizotypal personality and borderline personality: The predictive power of prayer. *Journal for the Scientific Study of Religion,* (ISSN: 1468-5906).

Burch, G.S.J., Pavelis, C., Hemsley, D.R., & Corr, P.J. (2006). Schizotypy and creativity in visual artists *British Journal of Psychology, 97,* 177–190.

Byrd, R.C. (1988). Positive therapeutic effects of intercessory prayer in a coronary care unit population. *Southern Medical Journal, 81,* 826-829.

Carlson, N.R. (2010). *Physiology of behaviour.* Boston, MA: Allyn & Bacon.

Chung, M.C., & Hyland, M. (2012). *History and philosophy of psychology.* Chichester: Wiley-Blackwell.

Claridge, G. (1997). *Schizotypy: Implications for illness and health.* Oxford University Press: Oxford.

Cohen, D. (2013). Freud and the British royal family. *The Psychologist, 26,* 462-463.

Corbett, L. (1966). *The religious function of the psyche.* London: Routledge.

Cronbach, L.J. (1951). Coefficient alpha and the internal structure of tests. *Psychometrika, 16*, 297-334.

CSO (2012a). Central statistics office: Population usually resident and present in the State by nationality, sex, religion and census year. Retrieved June 16, 2012, from http://www.cso.ie/en/media/csoie/releasespublications /documents/labourmarket/2012/qnhs_q12012.pdf

CSO (2012b). Central statistics office: Material compiled and presented by the Central Statistics Office. Retrieved June 16, 2012, from http://www.cso.ie/en/media/csoie/census/documents/v ol12_entire.pdf

Davey, G. (2008). *Psychopathology: Research, assessment and treatment in clinical psychology.* Chichester: Wiley-Blackwell.

Davies, E., & Burdett, J. (2004). Preventing 'schizophrenia': Creating the conditions for saner societies. In J. Read, L.R. Mosher, & R.P. Bentall (Eds.) (2004), *Models of madness: Psychological, social and biological approaches to schizophrenia* (pp. 271-282). Hove: Routledge.

Dawkins, R. (2006). *The God delusion.* London: Transworld Publishers.

References

Day, S., & Peters, E.R. (1999). The incidence of schizotypy in New Religious Movements. *Personality & Individual Differences, 27*, 55-67.

Diduca, D., & Joseph, S. (1997). Schizotypal traits and dimensions of religiosity. *British Journal of Clinical Psychology, 36,* 635-638.

Ellison, C.G. (1995). Race, religious involvement and depressive symptomatology in a southeastern U.S. community. *Social Science and Medicine, 40,* 1561-1572.

Ellison, C.G., Boardman, J.D., Williams, D.R., & Jackson, J.S. (2001). Religious involvement, stress and mental health: Findings from the 1995 Detroit area study. *Social Forces, 80,* 215-249.

Ewen, R.B. (1993). *An introduction to theories of personality.* London: Lawrence Erlbaum Associates.

Folley, B.S., & Park, S. (2005). Verbal creativity and schizotypal personality in relation to prefrontal hemispheric laterality: A behavioral and near-infrared optical imaging study. *Schizophrenia Research, 80,* 271-282.

Fonseca-Pedora, E., Lemos-Giraldez, S., Muniz, J., Garcia-Cueto, E., & Campillo-Alvarez, A. (2008). Schizotypy in adolescence: The role of gender and age. *The Journal of Nervous and Mental Disease, 196,* 161-165.

Fonseca-Pedora, E., Paino, M., Lemos-Giraldez, S., Garcia-Cueto, E., Campillo-Alvarez, A., Villazon-Garcia, U., & Muniz, J. (2008). Schizotypy assessment: State of the art and future prospects. *International Journal of Clinical and Health Psychology, 8,* 577-593.

Francis, L.J., & Evans, T.E. (1996). The relationship between personal prayer and purpose in life among churchgoing and non-churchgoing twelve-to-fifteen-year-olds in the UK. *Religious Education, 91,* 9-21.

Francis, L.J., & Gibbs, D. (1996). Prayer and self-esteem among 8- to 11-year-olds in the United Kingdom. *The Journal of Social Psychology, 136,* 791-793.

Francis, L.J., & Kaldor, P. (2002). The relationship between psychological well-being and Christian faith and practice in an Australian sample. *Journal for the Scientific Study of Religion, 41,* 179-184.

References

Francis, L.J., Robbins, M., Lewis, C.A., Quigley, C.F., & Wheeler, C. (2004). Religiosity and general health among undergraduate students: A response to O'Connor, Cobb, and O'Connor (2003). *Personality and Individual Differences, 37*, 485-494.

Freud, S (1949). *The future of an illusion.* London: The Hogarth Press.

Galton, F. (1872). Statistical inquiries into the efficacy of prayer. *Fortnightly Review, 12*, 125-135.

Geekie, J. (2004). Listening to the voices we hear: Clients' understanding of psychotic's experiences. In J. Read, L.R. Mosher, & R.P. Bentall (Eds.) (2004), *Models of madness: Psychological, social and biological approaches to schizophrenia* (pp. 147-160). Hove: Routledge.

Gross, R. (1996). *Psychology: The science of mind and behaviour.* London: Hodder & Stoughton.

Hall, J., Francis, L., & Callaghan, B. (2011). Faith and psychology in historical dialogue. *The Psychologist, 24*, (4) 260-262.

Harrison, P. (1995). Schizophrenia: A misunderstood disease. *Psychology Review, 2*, 2-6.

Hefti, R. (2009). Integrating spiritual issues into therapy. In P. Huguelet & H.G. Koenig (Eds.) (2009), *Religion and Spirituality in Psychiatry,* (pp. 244-267). New York: Cambridge University Press.

Heinrichs, R.W. (1993). Schizophrenia and the brain: Conditions for a neuropsychology of madness. *American Psychologist, 48,* 221-233.

Hewitt, J.K., & Claridge, G. (1989). The factor structure of schitzotypy in a normal population. *Personality and Individual Differences, 10,* 323-329.

Hill, P.C., & Hood, R.W. (1999). A preliminary note on measurement and scales in the psychology of religion. In P.C. Hill & R.W. Hood (Eds.) (1999), *Measures of Religiosity.* Birmingham, AL: Religious Education Press.

Hill, P.C., Pargament, K.I., Hood, R.W., McCullough, M.E., Swyers, J.P., Larson, D.B., & Zinnbauer, B.J. (2000). Conceptualizing religion and spirituality: Points of commonality, points of departure. *Journal for the Theory of Social Behaviour, 30,* 51-77.

Hirschle, J. (2009). Ireland`s economic miracle and its
religious decline: A consumption-oriented
interpretation. Retrieved June 20, 2012, from
http://www.fernuni-
hagen.de/imperia/md/content/soziologie/soz4/hasg_9.
pdf

Holder, D.W., DuRant, R.H., Harris, T.L., Henderson, D, J.,
Obeidallah, D., & Goodman, E. (2000). The
association between adolescent spirituality and
voluntary sexual activity. *Journal of Adolescent
Health, 26,* 295-302.

Hood, R.W., Spilka, B., Hunsberger B., & Gorsuch R.
(1996). *The psychology of religion: An empirical
approach.* New York, NY: The Guildford Press.

Hope A. (2009). A standard drink in Ireland: What strength?
Health Service Executive – Alcohol Implementation
Group. Retrieved June 20, 2012, from
http://www.yourdrinking.ie/reports/HPR00520.pdf

Horrigan, B., & Krucoff, M.W. (1999). The Mantra study
project. *Alternative Therapies, 5,* 75-82.

Huguelet, P., & Mohr, S. (2009). Religion/spirituality and
psychosis. In P. Huguelet & H.G. Koenig (Eds.)
(2009), *Religion and Spirituality in Psychiatry,* (pp.
65-80). New York: Cambridge University Press.

Hull, J.M. (2002). Spiritual development: Interpretations and applications. *British Journal of Religious Education, 24*, 171-182.

Jackson, M. (1997). Benign schizotypy? The case of spiritual experience. In G. Claridge (Ed.) (1997), *Schizotypy: Implications for illness and health* (pp. 227-250). Oxford: Oxford University Press.

James, W. (1985). *The varieties of religious experience.* Cambridge: Harvard University Press.

Joseph, J. (2004). Schizophrenia and heredity: Why the emperor has no genes. In J. Read, L.R. Mosher, & R.P. Bentall (Eds.) (2004), *Models of madness: Psychological, social and biological approaches to schizophrenia* (pp. 21-34). Hove: Routledge.

Joseph, S., & Diduca, D. (2001). Schizotypy and religiosity in 13-18 year old school pupils. *Mental Health, Religion & Culture, 5,* 63-69.

Joseph, S., Smith, D., & Diduca, D. (2002). Religious orientation and its association with personality, schizotypal traits and manic-depressive experiences. *Mental Health, Religion & Culture, 5,* 73-81.

Joyce, C.R.B., & Weldon, R.M.C. (1965). The objective efficacy of prayer: A double blind clinical trial. *Journal of Chronic Diseases, 18,* 367-377.

Jung, C.G. (1938). *Psychology and religion*. New Haven, CT: Yale University Press.

Jung, C.G. (2001). *Modern man in search of a soul.* London: Routledge.

Keane, C. (2009). *Going home: Irish stories from the edge of death.* Bray: Capel Island.

Kendler, K.S., Gardner, C.O., & Prescott, C.A. (1997). Religion, psychopathology, and substance use and abuse: A multimeasure, genetic-epidemiologic study. *The American Journal of Psychiatry, 154,* 322-329.

Kerns, J.G. (2006). Schizotypy facets, cognitive control, and emotion. *Journal of Abnormal Psychology, 115,* 418-427.

Kline, P. (1986). *A handbook of test construction: Introduction to psychometric design.* London: Methuen.

Knabb, J.J., & Newgren, K.P. (2011). The craftsman and his apprentice: A Kohutian interpretation of the Gospel narratives of Jesus Christ. *Pastoral Psychology, 60,* 245-262.

Koenig, H. G. (2009). Religion, spirituality and consultation-liaison psychiatry. In P. Huguelet & H.G. Koenig (Eds.) (2009), *Religion and Spirituality in Psychiatry,* (pp. 190-214). New York: Cambridge University Press.

Koenig, H.G., Ford, S.M., George, L.K., Blazer, D.G., & Meador, K.G. (1993). Religion and anxiety disorder: An examination and comparison of associations in young, middle-aged, and elderly. *Journal of Anxiety Disorders, 7,* 321-342.

Koenig, H.G., Hays, J.C., George, L.K., Blazer, D.G., Larson, D.B., & Landerman, L.R. (1997). Modeling the cross-sectional relationship between religion, physical health, social support, and depressive symptoms. *The American Journal of Geriatric Psychiatry, 5,* 131-143.

Kogan, J.N., Edelstein, B.A., & McKee, D.R. (2000). Assessment of anxiety in older adults: Current status. *Journal of Anxiety Disorders, 14,* 109-132.

Kohut, H. (1977). *The restoration of the self.* Madison, WI: International University Press.

Kowalski, R. & Westen, D. (2011). *Psychology.* Hoboken, NJ: Wiley.

References

Krucoff, M.W., Crater, S.W., Green, C.L., Mass, A.C., Seskevich, J.E., Lane, J.D., Loeffler, K.A., Morris, K., Bashore, T.M., & Koenig, H.G. (2001). Integrative noetic therapies as adjuncts to percutaneous intervention during unstable coronary syndromes: Monitoring and actualization of noetic training (MANTRA) feasibility pilot. *American Heart Journal, 142,* 760-767.

Kurtz, E., & Ketcham, K. (2002). *The spirituality of imperfection: Storytelling and the search for meaning.* New York, NY: Bantam Books.

Ladd, K. L., & Spilka, B. (2002). Inward, outward, and upward: Cognitive aspects of prayer. *Journal for the Scientific Study of Religion, 41,* 475-484.

Laing, R.D. (1990). *The divided self: An existential study in sanity and madness.* London: Penguin.

Lenington, S. (1979). Effects of holy water on the growth of radish plants. *Psychological Reports, 45,* 381-382.

Lesmana, C.B., & Tiliopoulos, N. (2009). Schizotypal personality traits and attitudes toward Hinduism among Balinese Hindus. *Mental Health, Religion & Culture, 12,* 773-785.

Levine, M. (2008). Prayer as coping: A psychological analysis. *Journal of Health and Chaplaincy, 15,* 80-98.

Lewis, C.A., Francis, L.J., & Enger, T. (2004). Personality, prayer and church attendance among a sample of 11 to 18 year olds in Norway. *Mental Health, Religion & Culture, 7,* 269-274.

Lewis, C.A., & Maltby, J. (1995). Religious attitude and practice: The relationship with obsessionality. *Personality and Individual Differences, 19,* 105-108.

Lickey M.E., & Gordon B. (1983). *Drugs for mental illness.* New York, NY: W.H. Freeman and Company.

Lindgren, K.N., & Coursey, R.D. (1995). Spirituality and serious mental illness: A two-part study. *Psychosocial Rehabilitation Journal, 18,* 93-111.

Loewenthal, K.M. (2000). *The psychology of religion: A short introduction.* Oxford: Oneworld Publications.

Loewenthal, K. (2007). *Religion, Culture and Mental Health.* Cambridge: Cambridge University Press.

MacLachlan, M., & Hand, K. (2013). *Happy nation? Prospects for psychological prosperity in Ireland.* Dublin: Liffey Press.

Malinowski, P. (2008). Mindfulness as psychological dimension: Concepts and applications. *The Irish Journal of Psychology, 29,* 155-166.

Maltby, J., & Day, L. (2002). Religious experience, religious orientation and schizotypy. *Mental Health, Religion & Culture, 5,* 163-174.

References

Maltby, J., Garner, I., Lewis, C.A., & Day, L. (2000). Religious orientatioin and schizotypal traits. *Personality and Individual Differences, 28,* 143-151.

Markides, K.S. (1983). Aging, religiosity, and adjustment: A longitudinal analysis. *Journal of Gerontology, 38,* 621-625.

Marler, P.L., & Hadaway C.K. (2002). "Being religious" or "being spiritual" in America: A zero-sum proposition? *Journal for the Scientific Study of Religion, 41,* 289-300.

Mason, O., & Claridge, G. (2006). The Oxford-Liverpool Inventory of Feelings and Experiences (O-Life): Further description and extended norms. *Schizophrenia Research, 82,* 203-211.

Mason, O., Claridge, G., & Jackson, M. (1995). New scales for the assessment of schizotypy. *Personality and Individual Differences, 18,* 7-13.

Mason, O., Linney, V., & Claridge, G. (2005). Short scales for measuring schizotypy. *Schizophrenia Research, 78,* 293-296.

Matthews, W.J., Conti, J.M., & Sireci, S.G. (2001). The effects of intercessory prayer, positive visualization and expectancy on the well-being of kidney dialysis patients. *Alternative Therapies, 7,* 42-52.

Mattis, J.S., Fontenot, D.W., & Hatcher-Kay, C.A. (2003). Religiosity, racism, and dispositional optimism among African Americans. *Personality and Individual Differences, 34,* 1025-1038.

Mercer, J.A. (2011). Vampires, desire, girls and God: Twilight and the spiritualties of adolescent girls. *Pastoral Psychology, 60,* 263-278.

Merkur, D. (1993). *Gnosis: An esoteric tradition of mystical visions and unions.* New York, NY: State University of New York Press.

Miller, L., & Kelly, B.S. (2005). Relationships of religiosity and spirituality with mental health and psychopathology. In R.F. Paloutzian & C.C. Park (Eds.) (2005), *Handbook of the Psychology of Religion* (pp. 460-478). London: The Guildford Press.

Mohr, S., & Huguelet, P. (2004). The relationship between schizophrenia and religion and its implications for care. *Swiss Medical Weekly, 134,* 369-376.

Mohr, S., & Pfeifer, S. (2009). Delusions and hallucinations with religious content. In P. Huguelet & H.G. Koenig (Eds.) (2009), *Religion and Spirituality in Psychiatry,* (pp. 81-96). New York: Cambridge University Press.

References

Mongan D., Reynolds S., Fanagan S., & Long J. (2007). *Health-related consequences of problem alcohol use. Overview 6.* Dublin: Health Research Board.

Morrison, A.P. (2004). Cognitive therapy for people with psychosis. In J. Read, L.R. Mosher, & R.P. Bentall (Eds.) (2004), *Models of madness: Psychological, social and biological approaches to schizophrenia* (pp. 291-306). Hove: Routledge.

Nettle, D. (2006). Schizotypy and mental health amongst poets, visual artists, and mathematicians. *Journal of Research in Personality, 40,* 876-890.

Nic Ghiolla Phádraig, M. (2009). Research update: Religion in Ireland: No longer an exception. Retrieved June 15, 2012, from http://www.ark.ac.uk/publications/updates/update64.pdf

Nonnmaker, J.M., McNeely, C.A., & Blum, R.W. (2003). Public and private domains of religiosity and adolescent health risk behaviors: Evidence from the national longitudinal study of adolescent health. *Social Science and Medicine, 57,* 2049-2054.

Norton, M.I., & Gino, F. (2013). Rituals alleviate grieving for loved ones, lovers, and lotteries. *Journal of Experimental Psychology: General.* Advance online publication. doi: 10.37/a0031772

O'Connor, D.B., Cobb, J., & O'Connor, R.C. (2003). Religiosity, stress and psychological distress: No evidence for an association among undergraduate students. *Personality and Individual Differences, 34,* 211-217.

O'Doherty, M. (2008). *Empty pulpits: Ireland's retreat from religion.* Dublin: Gill & Macmillan.

O'Reilly, T., Dunbar, R., & Bental, R. (2001). Schizotypy and creativity: An evolutionary connection. *Personality and Individual Differences, 31,* 1067-1078.

Perroud, N. (2009). Religion/spirituality and neuropsychiatry. In P. Huguelet & H.G. Koenig (Eds.) (2009), *Religion and Spirituality in Psychiatry,* (pp. 48-64). New York: Cambridge University Press.

Peters, E., Day, S., McKenna, J., & Orbach, G. (1999). Delusional ideation in religious and psychotic populations. *British Journal of Clinical Psychology, 38,* 83-96.

Piedmont, R. L. (2009). Personality, spirituality, religiousness, and the personality disorders: Predictive relations and treatment implications. In P. Huguelet & H.G. Koenig (Eds.) (2009), *Religion and Spirituality in Psychiatry,* (pp. 173-189). New York: Cambridge University Press.

References

Poloma, M. M., & Pendleton, B. F. (1991). The effects of prayer and prayer experiences on measures of general well-being. *Journal of Psychology and Theology, 19*, 71-83.

Rawlings, D., Claridge, G., & Freeman, J.L. (2001). Principal components analysis of the Schizotypal Personality Scale (STA) and the Borderline Personality Scale (STB). *Personality and Individual Differences, 31*, 409-419.

Read, J. (2004a). A history of madness. In J. Read, L.R. Mosher, & R.P. Bentall (Eds.) (2004), *Models of madness: Psychological, social and biological approaches to schizophrenia* (pp. 9-20). Hove: Routledge.

Read, J. (2004b). The invention of 'schizophrenia'. In J. Read, L.R. Mosher, & R.P. Bentall (Eds.) (2004), *Models of madness: Psychological, social and biological approaches to schizophrenia* (pp. 21-34). Hove: Routledge.

Read, J. (2004c). Biological psychiatry's lost cause. In J. Read, L.R. Mosher, & R.P. Bentall (Eds.) (2004), *Models of madness: Psychological, social and biological approaches to schizophrenia* (pp. 57-65). Hove: Routledge.

Read, J. (2004d). Does 'schizophrenia' exist? In J. Read, L.R. Mosher, & R.P. Bentall (Eds.) (2004), *Models of madness: Psychological, social and biological approaches to schizophrenia* (pp. 44-53). Hove: Routledge.

Read, J. (2004e). Poverty, ethnicity and gender. In J. Read, L.R. Mosher, & R.P. Bentall (Eds.) (2004), *Models of madness: Psychological, social and biological approaches to schizophrenia* (pp. 161-194). Hove: Routledge.

Read, J. & Haslam, N. (2004). Public opinion: Bad things happen and can drive you crazy. In J. Read, L.R. Mosher, & R.P. Bentall (Eds.) (2004), *Models of madness: Psychological, social and biological approaches to schizophrenia* (pp. 36-42). Hove: Routledge.

Read, J. & Mason, J. (2004). Genetics, eugenics and mass murder. In J. Read, L.R. Mosher, & R.P. Bentall (Eds.) (2004), *Models of madness: Psychological, social and biological approaches to schizophrenia* (pp. 36-42). Hove: Routledge.

References

Read, J., Mosher, L.R., & Bentall, R.P. (2004). 'Schizophrenia' is not an illness. In J. Read, L.R. Mosher, & R.P. Bentall (Eds.) (2004), *Models of madness: Psychological, social and biological approaches to schizophrenia* (pp. 3-8). Hove: Routledge.

Reedy, A.R., & Kobayashi, R. (2012). Substance use and mental health disorders: Why do some people suffer from both? *Social Work in Mental Health, 10,* 496-517. DOI: 10.1080/15332985.2012.709480

Ricard, M. (2007). *Happiness: A guide to developing life's most important skill.* London: Atlantic Books.

Scheper-Hughes, N. (2001). *Saints, scholars, and schizpohrenics: Mental illness in Rural Ireland.* London: University of California Press.

Scherman, K. (1981). *The flowering of Ireland: Saints, scholars and kings.* Boston, MA: Little, Brown and Company.

Schumaker, J.F. (1995). *The corruption of reality: A unified theory of religion, hypnosis, and psychopathology.* New York, NY: Prometheus Books.

Schuman, W. (2003). *The big book of angels.* Dingly, Australia: Hinkler Books Pty Ltd.

Seligman, M.E.P. (2002). *Authentic happiness: Using the new positive psychology to realize your potential for lasting fulfillment.* New York, NY: The Free Press.

Sherkat, D.E., & Reed, M.D. (1992). The effects of religion and social support on self-esteem and depression among the suddenly bereaved. *Social Indicators Research, 26,* 259-275.

Shevlin, M., Dorahy, M. Adamson, G., & Murphy, J. (2007). Subtypes of borderline personality disorder, associated clinical disorders and stressful life-events: A latent class analysis based on the British Psychiatric Morbidity Survey. *British Journal of Clinical Psychology, 46,* 273-281.

Strayhorn, J.M., Weidman, C.S., & Larson, D. (1990). A measure of religiousness, and its relation to parent and child mental health variables. *Journal of Community Psychology, 18,* 34-43.

The Schizophrenia Commission (2012). *The abandoned illness: a report from the Schizophrenia Commission.* London: Rethink Mental Illness.

Tiliopoulos, N., & Bikker, A. (2013). A thematic comparison of religiosity profiles between Christians with low and high schizotypy. *Mental Health, Religion & Culture, 16*, 173-178.

Ulanov, A. (1997). Jung and religion: The opposing Self. In P. Young-Eisendrath & T. Dawson (Eds.) (1997), *The Cambridge companion to Jung* (pp. 296-313). Cambridge: Cambridge University Press.

Unterrainer, H.F., Huber, H.P., Sorgo, I.M., Collicutt, J., & Fink, A. (2011). Dimensions of religious/spiritual well-being and schizotypal personality. *Personality and Individual Differences, 51,* 360-364.

Walsh, D., & Daly, A. (2004). Mental illness in Ireland 1750-2002: Reflections on the rise and fall of institutional care. Retrieved July 7, 2012, from http://www.hrb.ie/uploads/tx_hrbpublications/Mental_Illness_in_Ireland.pdf

Watts, A.W. (1962). *The way of zen.* Middlesex: Penguin.

Whelan, C. (1994). Social class, unemployment, and psychological distress. *European: Sociological Review, 10,* 49-61.

White, J. (1990). *Kundalini evolution and enlightenment.* New York, NY: Paragon House.

White, J., Joseph, S., & Neil, A. (1995). Religiosity, psychoticism, and schizotypal traits. *Personality and Individual Differences, 19,* 847-851.

Wilson, W. P. (2009). Psychiatric treatments involving religion: Psychotherapy from a Christian perspective. In P. Huguelet & H.G. Koenig (Eds.) (2009), *Religion and Spirituality in Psychiatry,* (pp. 283-300). New York: Cambridge University Press.

Zohar, D., & Marshall, I. (2000). *SQ spiritual intelligence the ultimate intelligence.* London: Bloomsbury.

Printed in Great Britain
by Amazon